STORRIE™

CREATING THE FUNCTIONAL MEDICINE REVOLUTION

COMPILED BY
DR. CHRISTINE MANUKYAN

Published by STORRIE™ Publishing

Copyright © 2022 Dr. Christine Manukyan

Editing and Ghostwriting by Danielle Damrell

Cover Design by Jennifer Rae and Danielle Damrell

ISBN: 9798429235837

*To those who have felt stuck, undervalued,
and overworked yet continue to overcome:
You are seen, heard, and needed. Your work is not in vain.*

*To those who have dedicated their lives to the
healthcare industry – Thank you for standing on the front lines
during unprecedented times, we honor you. You are saving lives.*

*Keep walking forward and soon you will discover the path
towards creating your own path and rewriting the chapter of your life
that helps you to align your mind, body, and spirit.*

*We all deserve a second chance to rewrite our story
and become the best version of ourselves.*

TABLE OF CONTENTS

ABOUT THE AUTHORS

By: Dr. Christine Manukyan

"The doctor of the future will give no medication but will instruct his patients in the care of the human frame, diet and in the cause and prevention of disease."

– THOMAS EDISON

When you make the decision to stop allowing fear to get in your way, you unlock the potential to change your life and the lives of those around you. When I left my job during the global pandemic in 2020 and started my entrepreneurial journey as a functional medicine practitioner and business coach, I visualized creating a tribe of clinicians who believed in functional medicine just as much as I did. I pictured the ways our lives would change forever as we stepped into a new chapter of our lives. I knew that it was possible, and I knew my tribe was out there somewhere.

The authors you will meet within the pages of this book are my tribe. They are the courageous healthcare professionals who have chosen to step out of a life riddled with burnout and into a purpose-filled life where balance is truly possible. Together, these authors are empowering others to reach their health goals without pharmaceuticals and to find real answers through using functional medicine. They have realized that it's time we create the FUNCTIONAL MEDICINE REVOLUTION and change lives around the world using the healing modalities that have existed forever – natural and holistic medicine. The stories the authors are sharing will serve as proof of their resilient spirits, and our hope is that you will be inspired by their journeys to take action and create the life you are worthy of living. This collaborative book is evidence that anyone can reclaim their power, unlock their impact, and unleash their full potential.

We are *CREATING THE FUNCTIONAL MEDICINE REVOLUTION!*

We are creating new and improved standards of practice so our patients and clients get the best care available.

We are creating a foundation for the future generation of clinicians who will have the opportunity to learn how to integrate functional medicine into every patient's care plan.

These authors have joined my mission to impact 1 million lives around the world with functional medicine. We are making an impact in this world, one life at a time.

They say, "If you build it, they will come." Brick by brick, I saw this to be true. And today I am excited and honored to be leading THE FUNCTIONAL MEDICINE REVOLUTION and to be creating opportunities for clinicians to become Certified Functional Medicine Specialists™ from The STORRIE™ Institute.

These authors have become my best friends and colleagues. We laugh together, we cry together, and we always have each other's back. Each author came into my life for a distinct reason. Individually, they have gone through a lot and until this moment, their experiences have been locked away within them, just waiting to be honored and shared. Now is the time for their stories to be unleashed and their impact to be felt across the world.

The Main Goal of **CREATING THE FUNCTIONAL MEDICINE REVOLUTION** is: To honor the stories shared so that their legacies can live on and help you unleash your own truth and continue to heal and grow from within. They all bring in their unique voices and gifts into The STORRIE™ Institute, and for that, I am forever grateful.

This is my tribe, and together we are ***CREATING THE FUNCTIONAL MEDICINE REVOLUTION.***

Live your passion,

Dr. Christine Manukyan | Founder & CEO The STORRIE™ Institute

To learn more about The STORRIE™ Institute,
go to www.storrieinstitute.com and join our private
Facebook community - Functional Medicine Business Coaching
For Clinicians

FOREWORD

By: Danielle Damrell

What if I told you that every trial, tragedy, and triumph we walk through is *necessary* in order to get to the place we all strive to be at? A place where peace, joy, and balance are not only possible but are a present reality. A place where your purpose is fulfilled and your heart is content. Well, my friend, that's the truth. It is necessary to walk through the good times and the bad to get to a good place, a great place in fact. I often wonder what it would be like if we were all just born into a life where every day was just a "good" day? During hard times that may seem like a relief and maybe that sounds ok to some, but to me, that sounds boring. Just a good day? No, thanks! I want great days! Days that are filled with laughter, spontaneity, and most importantly, real connection and purpose-driven impact. I know for a fact that this type of life is possible, and I also know that it takes a lot of determination to make it happen.

Every day, from the moment we wake up, we are bombarded with choices. From snoozing the alarm clock to brushing your teeth. How about makeup or no makeup? How about the bigger choices we face like getting married, having children, or choosing a career field? The choices are endless. There is a time and a season for everything in life, and the decisions we make each and every day determine the kind of life we create for ourselves. You never really know where life is going to take you, and you can't change where you have been or what you have already gone through. I can tell you one thing for sure though, our pasts will never have the power to dictate who we are because every day we have the opportunity to choose to rewrite our stories.

As you read this book, I would love for you to keep one question in mind: Am I going to keep pressing snooze, or am I ready to wake up and experience the life I was created to live?

The authors of this book have made the decision to wake up! It is an honor to be writing the foreword for this book and this opportunity is nothing short of a miracle, and not just for me. I have had the privilege of getting to know each one of the authors personally because I am serving as the Creative Director for the STORRIE™ Institute and have edited this book from start to finish. I have walked with them through this whole process, from creating an outline to meeting with each of them to go over final revisions. To me, this isn't just a job. This is a fulfillment of the mission and call I've had on my life for many years– the call to amplify and lift up the stories of those around me. My prayer is that throughout the course of this book, these stories will bring clarity and life-changing encouragement to each one of you reading this.

Every author in this book needed their paths to line up perfectly for them to be sharing their stories through the pages within this book, many of which are doing so for the very first time. This is the moment so many of us have dreamed of, but weren't sure how it could ever possibly happen. I've heard it said before that over 50% of people have the desire to write a book, yet, only 2% actually do it. Let's talk for a moment about why that is. The truth is, writing and editing a book is hard. Publishing one is a process that most people don't even begin to know how to navigate. Okay, it's a little easier when you're co-authoring a collaborative book like this one, but it's still a big task to accomplish. The efforts are not in vain, however, because the end result is a beautiful book that holds a snapshot into the lives and experiences that are ready to be shared and read for generations to come.

Creating the Functional Medicine Revolution is not just any book, nope, not at all. This book is a powerful collection of true stories that are a peek into the lives of 15 incredible women who have made the courageous decision to say, "No more!" to the unnecessary dysfunction within our conventional medical system. Every one of these authors has gone through copious amounts of schooling only to realize that the jobs into which they have entered have limited their capacity for real impact. Throughout the course of this book, you will read story after story about how their passion to heal and serve others turned into a vicious cycle of working insanely long days, experiencing burnout, and treating reversible conditions with a band-aid, all while sacrificing their own health. You will find that through it all, they have persevered and their determination to provide real healing care to people is only stronger now. These stories will serve as proof that this revolution needed to take place for far too long, and now is the time.

Now is the time to CREATE the functional medicine revolution. The principles of functional medicine have existed since the beginning of time. Before we had the technological advances we have now, humans only had natural options to treat pain. Let me get something perfectly clear, every one of us who is a part of this movement is well aware that conventional, Western medicine still serves a great purpose. In fact, many of the authors still work in the conventional medicine field, while simultaneously treating patients on a 1:1 basis through their own practices. Conventional medicine is great for treating acute symptoms, and it saves lives every day through surgeries and medications that allow one's body to continue functioning enough to stay alive. Functional medicine offers more for people, however. Instead of just "staying alive", functional medicine offers the opportunity to actually heal our bodies from within and thrive! Chronic illnesses are not given the "just live with it" answer and when acute symptoms arise, the answer is not "here's a pill" but rather, "Why is this really happening? What's really causing this problem?" You see, the "answers" patients are often given within the traditional treatment model do not actually provide real answers. Throughout the course of this book, you will have the opportunity to experience what it's like for people to find real answers and what type of work and decisions they made to make real healing possible for themselves and for their clients. By the end, you will understand why every day, conventional medicine practitioners are leaving their jobs to become functional medicine specialists.

The structure of this book is intentional. There are 15 chapters, one for each author. At the end of each chapter, you will find a bio, in which you can read more about how every clinician is serving at the time this book was published (March 2022). The chapters carry the powerful words of their life's stories and are paired with their professional bios. Both of these sections within the book will give you a complete view of the lives, missions, and hearts of each author. The reason for this is simple. If you are a practitioner yourself, we hope these stories encourage you to take back control of your life and make the impact that you are created to make. If you are a civilian like me, this book gives you great insight into what's going on behind the scenes in our medical system through the eyes of the people who know it best, medical doctors, pharmacists, nurses, and all other types of healthcare professionals. This also can serve as a quick reference manual to find real healing for those suffering from chronic illnesses or annoying symptoms like headaches, anxiety, stomach issues, or pretty much any other uncomfortable (and abnormal) feeling that we humans far too often just learn to live with. These clinicians are ready to help you find real healing and get to the root cause of what has held you back from living a life filled with peace, joy, and purpose.

We are created for more, and that's exactly what functional medicine offers. More life, more peace, more joy, more healing, and more purpose than you ever could have imagined. It's time to rewrite your story and choose the life you were created to live.

— DANIELLE DAMRELL

ABOUT DANIELLE DAMRELL

Danielle Damrell is the Creative Director, Publication and Ghost Writer, and Chief Editor for *The STORRIE™ Institute.* Danielle is also a highly recognized lettering artist, graphic designer, wife, and mom. Her art has been featured worldwide, and she has been a featured author in publications including Business Insider, Forbes, Voyage Denver, and several other national publications.

In 2020 Danielle realized that the act of creative processing was a powerful key to unlocking the healing that she has always longed for. Coming from a background riddled with abuse, trauma, physical illness, an unexpected pregnancy, and mental health struggles, Danielle realized that it was up to her to break the cycle of chaos and dysfunction.

Beating all statistical odds, Danielle is now empowering and inspiring other women to step into the life of freedom and healing they are worthy of living. She has become an expert in creative processing and is often teaching others how to channel the pain and chaos of life into creating meaningful work. In 2021, she launched the Created Worthy Podcast and has created a platform for people from a wide variety of backgrounds and experiences to come and share their own life stories while they uncover the threads of creative processing that exists in each one of our lives already.

Danielle has been on a journey of uncovering her creative zone of expertise since 2017 when she founded the *Danielle Damrell Creative Collective*. Her business is a continuously expanding collection of creative services, motivation, products, playlists, and resources that aim to spread vulnerable encouragement and truth. Her faith has also played a major role in her healing journey, and she is frequently found sharing on social media about seeing daily miracles and maintaining balance (or at least what it looks like to try). Danielle knows first-hand the healing power of creative processing and equips others with the knowledge of how to utilize it as a skill and processing method in their own lives.

Danielle is now empowering and inspiring others to step into the life of freedom and healing that we are all worthy of living. Leaning on her personal and professional experiences, she is often found mentoring and teaching others how to channel the ups and downs of entrepreneurship, into creating meaningful work through focusing on intention. Within The STORRIE™ Institute, she also serves as an accountability advisor and creative coach for clinicians within the institute. Danielle's goal when working with clinicians specifically is to equip them with the structure and support needed to build a sustainable functional medicine practice that is free from overwhelm and burnout.

Danielle is on a mission to inspire others to find joy in the midst of chaos.

www.damrellcreativeco.com | danielle@damrellcreativeco.com | Instagram: @danielledamrell | Facebook: @damrellcreativeco

Chapter 1

REWRITING MY STORY

By: Dr. Christine Manukyan, PharmD, MS

*"Everyone deserves a second chance to rewrite their story
and become the best version of themselves."*

– Dr. Christine Manukyan

In 2020, a year filled with endless unknowns, I walked away from the career I was building for over 20 years. On my 40th birthday, I became a corporate dropout. I was exhausted from the demands of working full-time and homeschooling (schools were closed due to the global pandemic) not to mention, trying to find childcare when my husband and I were working. I spent the majority of 2020 on the front lines as a hospital pharmacist in one of the busiest hospitals in the nation. By September, I had enough. I made the decision to leave my job and reclaim my life by diving headfirst into the world of functional medicine, instead. I was no longer willing to accept the fact that the medications I was handing to my patients were only a temporary solution to their deep-rooted problems. I knew that there was a better way, and I was willing to do whatever it took to help people find real healing. This decision led to the first chapter in my pursuit to rewrite my story.

My decision to leave was the first step of unleashing the story that was trapped inside my visionary mind for far too long. Within a year of becoming a corporate dropout, I celebrated my first ever 6-figure month. I had changed the narrative of "I'm just a pharmacist" to "I am Dr. Christine Manukyan and I am leading the Functional Medicine Revolution." Big shift, isn't it? Well, I would be lying if I said it was a smooth and easy transition, but with grit, hard work, and determination, it is possible! And I know that for a fact.

You may be asking, "How did someone with a strictly clinical background accomplish all these unconventional tasks so quickly?" The truth is, I did not go to school for business, I had no experience with entrepreneurship, nor did I attend school for functional medicine. Nevertheless, my vision, my life and my experiences have guided me to the place I am today. My own health transformation journey opened up several opportunities to talk about my story, learn and teach about functional medicine, and thus paved the way for my entrepreneurial voyage. I finally have the opportunity to dream again, live my life with intention and purpose, and help other practitioners to do the same. This is the beginning of the functional medicine revolution the medical community has needed for far too long.

Our stories are an evolutionary process. We become who we are through our childhood experiences and the choices we make as we grow up. I was a first-generation Armenian American. At just 16 years old, I moved to the United States, excited about the future ahead. One of the first things I had to get used to, the "American diet." I didn't know about things like processed food, GMOs, artificial colors and sweeteners, chemicals, preservatives, pesticides and all the other stuff that is often found in our food. When I was growing up, I remember my grandparents always using home remedies whenever we caught a cold or flu, and they rarely used any medications to treat anything. Organic food was all I knew because, back home during the 80s, that's all we had. Organic fresh food was our nutrition and our medicine. I drank water from the water faucet without thinking twice about if it had any additional chemicals, and I would eat butter every day without worrying about cholesterol. We would walk everywhere, occasionally take public transportation, but I was constantly active and moving my body because that was just part of our culture. We shopped at farmers markets and ate fruits and vegetables that were in season. Looking back, I realize we grew up with an ideal healthy lifestyle that was easy to take for granted.

It didn't take long for me to experience the effects of the crappy and cheap fast food I consumed as a teenager. The more I ate, the more I realized how sick my body was becoming. I found myself gaining weight, struggling with energy, and having a hard time focusing. This was not normal for me. Ultimately, my diet and lifestyle were affecting my mood, self-esteem, and my self-worth. My family couldn't afford to purchase organic food, as we were living paycheck to paycheck and received government assistance at the time. We could only afford cheap fast food that had absolutely no nutritional value and was just filled with crap.

If you grew up in the United States, you probably know exactly what I'm talking about. In fact, if you were raised in this western culture, you may only know American lifestyle as your norm. As someone who was new to this environment, however, I had no idea of the long term health issues this traditional "American diet" can cause. Growing up as a teenager, I was just trying to just fit in. I acclimated to this new lifestyle and little did I know, this would lead me to a variety of health challenges when I entered my 30s. The bad eating and exercise habits continued through my time in undergraduate and pharmacy school. I remember drinking 3 to 4 cans of diet soda each day, adding 5 to 7 packets of Splenda into my coffee, and eating ramen noodles filled with soy, sodium and GMOs. I would think to myself, "I am young, I don't have any health issues, so why not?" And when you add stress on top of a poor lifestyle, you may not know it, but you are speeding up the natural aging process.

Like many others, I was trading my health for potential wealth and was focused on achieving the "American dream." I worked hard throughout pharmacy school and graduated with honors while being class president and leader of several organizations. I was also working part-time at a retail pharmacy, but to be honest, it was rough. After graduating from Nova Southeastern University College of Pharmacy, I found myself constantly chasing the next big thing. For me, this looked like moving to Ohio from Florida and living alone for the first time while completing a 2-year residency at The Ohio State University Medical Center. I was also working on my master's degree in Health-System Pharmacy Administration. Needless to say, there was a lot on my plate and my personal health was not a priority at the time.

Within months of graduating from residency, I married my high school sweetheart, who also happened to become a hospital pharmacist. We quickly started our family and had 2 children. Having back-to-back pregnancies while working full time at the hospital, also took a huge toll on my health. I was still chasing the next big thing. I was chasing after promotions at work and chasing after the unrealistic idea that I could be the "perfect" wife and mom. In no time, I found myself living my life on autopilot and again, it took a huge toll on my body. While I was climbing the leadership ladder at work, I was slowly dying inside. Plus, back-to-back pregnancies caused more weight gain and spiraled my health completely out of control. As a new mother, I was focused on my family, work, and others. I forgot all about self-love and self-care. I was morbidly obese and saw my health declining as my career was seemingly blooming.

My energy was almost nonexistent, however, and I was unable to be fully present with my kids. I knew I could not continue like this, but I didn't know how much of a dire health situation I had gotten myself into.

In 2015, at 35 years old, I scheduled my annual checkup. At this appointment, I was told by my primary care physician that I was going to have a heart attack in the next 5 years if I continued with the lifestyle I had been living. I mean, who wants to hear they are going to die by age 40? That was scary, but the truth was I was morbidly obese, extremely burnt out, had high cholesterol, low energy, insomnia, brain fog, unexplained inflammation, and was under never-ending stress. I can honestly say I was a hot mess mamma who was just trying to take care of my two little ones while also working full time at a management level, which was increasingly more stressful. From the outside, I looked fine and I definitely didn't look "sick."

During that office visit with my primary care doctor, I was given a pill to lower my cholesterol, and I was told to go "lose some weight." Nothing was explained and I wasn't given any guidance on how to go about losing weight or if there were any other options out there to help to improve my health. As a pharmacist, I knew I was just being prescribed a toxic pill that was known to have many side effects. I was stunned and humiliated. I blamed myself and kept thinking, "I should have known better." I was confused and felt as if I had lost part of my identity.

I walked out of that 10-minute doctor's appointment so disappointed. Not only was I told I was going to die soon if I didn't make changes right away but I had also waited 6 months to even see the doctor and once I arrived, I waited over an hour before the doctor came into the room. My experience from start to finish was terrible. After the appointment, I sat in my car crying and began to feel increasingly more anxious about how I was going to fix this. I was overwhelmed and terrified at the thought of not being around to watch my children grow. I just knew there had to be a better way to reclaim my health without the toxic little pill I had been told to take.

This appointment had me spinning. I wanted to know why, as a patient, I was left to feel this way. Why wasn't my doctor asking me how I felt about taking this prescription? Why wasn't she having a conversation with me about what else I could do to lower my cholesterol? After all, according to my labs, it was only my cholesterol that was the problem. This also caused me to wonder why my doctor didn't even ask me how I am. If I was asked how I was really feeling, I would have shared that I was burnt out, overwhelmed, and overall, was not ok. The reality is, routine labs don't always tell the story of how a person is feeling, they just don't.

Without even realizing it, I had been sitting in my car for over an hour thinking about what had just happened. I had to gather my strength and pull myself together so I could drive home and face the reality that I wasn't prepared to face. As I was driving, I kept praying and manifesting for someone to come into my life who could help me. I needed someone who could be my accountability buddy to help me lose weight without starving myself. I had failed so many diets in the past, and I was tired of the unsuccessful dieting attempts that led me nowhere near being "healthy." I knew a decision needed to be made, so I started researching and gave myself time to discover a better way to lower my cholesterol and lose weight.

It was time for me to make a decision that would change my life forever. The choice I faced was either to settle and just take the pill, or I could challenge myself to look for an alternative. Spoiler alert, I chose option two. I focused my energy looking for alternative ways to heal my body. Taking care of my health suddenly became my top priority. After several weeks of searching, I found a solution. My friend and colleague introduced me to the realm of holistic health and led me towards receiving the best Mother's Day present I could have ever given myself. On Mother's Day in 2015 (May 11, 2015), I committed to rewriting my story in order to become the best version of myself. This season of my life was the beginning of something big. If my life was a book, 2015 would be the forward – *Choosing To Rewrite My Story.*

This commitment led me straight in the direction of functional medicine. I soon began focusing more on uncovering the root cause of my failing health and relearning how to use food as medicine. I realized my health was interconnected with my highly stressful career, so I made the decision to step down from my management position to work in hopes of bringing down my stress levels. This was a very hard decision to make, especially since this was the first time after all these years I would no longer be the "boss." I knew this was all a part of rewriting my story and reclaiming life though, so it was time for me to focus on what mattered the most to me – my health and my family. Putting aside my ego and title to focus on a healthy lifestyle was incredibly challenging, but worth it. For the first time in my life, I had to really ask myself, "How am I really doing?" Being "fine" or just "ok" was not good enough for me. I needed time to go back to the basics. For over 16 years, I lived an unhealthy lifestyle, so it would take determination to not fall back into the same habits I had become accustomed to.

Fast-forward six months and I was at a follow-up appointment with my same primary care doctor. My doctor wanted to make sure my labs were ok because I was supposed to start taking the cholesterol-lowering medication. I intentionally didn't say anything about not taking the medication, as I wanted to see if the lifestyle I had made would reflect in my lab work. I can remember this moment so clearly, my doctor walked in the room and told me "I think there is a lab error, we might have to redo your labs. Your labs are normal and I don't think the medication works that fast." I smiled at her and said, "There was no lab error, what you're looking at is the power of using food as medicine, incorporating adaptogens for stress management and natural energy, cellular cleansing, and intermittent fasting." I had also lost 35 pounds of toxic visceral fat, the fat that was surrounding my organs and causing all the health issues I was previously experiencing. I then started to share with her what changes I had been making over the last 6 months. My doctor was so impressed and asked me to send her more information so she could share it with her other patients. She even asked me if I was ok with her connecting me to others who would like to learn more about a holistic lifestyle. I got the green light from her to continue what I was doing. That one decision to change my health without pharmaceuticals and instead incorporate functional medicine became the catalyst of my life transformation journey, which later on became my passion, mission, and calling.

After experiencing my own health transformation using functional medicine, I realized the power that comes from making better decisions and how one decision can transform your entire life. My desire to chase the next big thing never went away, but instead of limiting myself to chase success through my job and unrealistic societal expectations, I decided to chase true success that started from within. Within my very own body. Over time, I went on to lose over 100 pounds through intermittent fasting, exercise, and incorporating functional medicine practices into my daily routine. I even experienced a boost of self-confidence that allowed me to step out on stage as a fitness competitor (bodybuilder). I stepped on stage as the real-life Wonder Woman, in order to empower other women to say "Yes!" to themselves and be an example of what's possible when you take consistent action. I also went on to run the LA Marathon on March 8th, 2020 – the very year that I would also turn 40. Mamma didn't have a heart attack like the doctor said, instead she ran a 26-mile marathon! When I crossed the finish line, I felt like I was the success story I had always hoped to become!

I became my first "client" using a holistic lifestyle to reach health goals, without realizing that my experiences would turn into my career just a few years later. For a while, I was still doing this as a "side gig" as I was still working full-time in the hospital and was not yet looking for an exit strategy. Well, that didn't last too long before I hit another rock bottom and found myself in the same exact place, confused and overwhelmed. I was, again, asking myself, "Is this it?" Is this what I am meant to be doing for the rest of my life until I retire? I felt so out of balance and unsettled because deep down, I knew I was meant for so much more. I just didn't know what it was going to look like until one day I heard a podcast that changed my life.

My commute used to take over 2 hours a day, most of which was spent sitting in traffic. I would often listen to podcasts to kill time. One evening, as I was driving home and trying to keep my eyes open after a very stressful evening shift at the hospital, I turned on a podcast where a Nurse Practitioner was sharing her story about how she went from traditional medicine into functional medicine and now has her own online practice. This happened to be the same day I was introduced to a master coach who worked alongside one of the most highly recognized business and life strategists in the nation. As I was listening to these women and their stories, I felt like they were speaking straight to my soul. I heard terms like "time freedom", "working from home", and "making a real impact in the world" for the very first time. I was eager to learn more, and started asking questions like, "How does an online practice work? What training and certifications are needed? Will the California Board of Pharmacy really allow me to have my own practice?" I mean, a million questions passed through my mind. These were all questions that I have never thought of asking myself, so it felt strange to even think about starting my own business. This was a huge investment, and I quickly started to question my ability to achieve these dreams of mine. The thought "What happens if I fail?" was top of mind.

It was January 2020, and something inside me switched on and suddenly my soul was on fire. I just knew this was going to be my year, no matter what. I knew that in order to make big, bold decisions, I needed to be surrounded by mentors and people who cheer me on and help me achieve my dreams. I needed a tribe that would elevate me so I could unleash my full potential! I invested in my very first personal development program with the coach I was introduced to and became a founding member of a tribe of badass business owners that they were building. At the same time, I also decided to hire my very first business coach and joined a mastermind, where I learned all about how to build a successful business from the ground up. During that mastermind, I met many women who have become some of my best friends.

I spent all year manifesting and preparing to leave my job by my 40th birthday. I dreamed and visualized creating my own functional medicine legacy. Like many people who make a pivot, I was so scared. I started doubting myself and questioning if I really knew enough to open my own practice. I was second-guessing myself and wondering if I made the right decision in hiring a business coach, someone I had just met. Then I remembered why I hired my business coach in the first place. I did this because my *why* was so strong. I no longer wanted to choose between my health, my family, and my career, and I knew it was possible to have freedom in all of these areas of life.

Once I was done with making excuses and waiting for the "right time", I got out of my own way and got to work. In March 2020, the global pandemic quickly proved that I was making the right investments and decisions for my life. The world was changing so quickly. Overnight, telemedicine and online virtual practice became the new normal. I quickly realized how much I had to learn and how fast I needed to implement everything I had been learning. As a clinical pharmacist, I was trained in the acute care hospital setting for 13 years, and now I had to shift my focus to preventative medicine using functional medicine. There was a tight deadline to get things in order because I was set to launch my practice in May. There was a lot on my plate, but I stayed laser-focused on my vision and nothing could distract me. I was like one of those racing horses with their side blinders on, running in one lane, fast and with intention. I learned how to own my worth and charge for my services and my consultations. All of this to become a business owner, functional medicine practitioner, and coach.

There was an opportunity in my profession as a pharmacist that many haven't thought about. I saw an opportunity for growth and an exit strategy if the pandemic was going to last longer than anticipated. Creating my own virtual functional medicine practice during the pandemic became my goal so I could fully walk away from the corporate world. I finally figured out the solution to my health, lifestyle, and career problems. I could now work from home as my own boss, without sacrificing my income, and I could do all this by launching my own virtual functional medicine practice. Once again, I felt so accomplished. I created something, without knowing exactly how it would happen, and let the desire to rewrite my story guide my way. I knew I would have many challenges along the way, and I was ok with that. It was a bold decision, and it was something that the real-life Wonder Woman would do, so I did it.

On May 11th, 2020 I launched my functional medicine practice. Crazy enough, this was exactly five years after starting my own health transformation journey. For a while, I continued working limited hours on the weekends at the hospital, in addition to my job. I realized that our childcare situation wasn't perfect, but we made it work as long as we could. Until, one day in late May, I was informed that my work schedule could not be accommodated any longer and that I needed to go back to work full-time starting in June. Telling our kids that we had to hire a nanny, a complete stranger from an agency, so I could go back to work, was one of the hardest days of my life. Both kids cried and asked questions like, "Why are you leaving us?", "What if this person hurts us?", "What if we get sick?", and "Why is work more important than us?" I cried as I tried to comfort them, saying things like "everything will be ok" and "we will get through this together." It was so hard and I couldn't sleep for many days in a row. I had to choose to go back to work, as working from home was not an option at the time, and I wasn't fully ready to leave my job. In my mind, I was still waiting for the perfect time to leave. I didn't have the mindset that was necessary in order to make big changes right at that moment. It was so hard, knowing I had no other options but to leave the kids and go back to work full-time.

Even though I had technically launched my functional medicine practice at the time, it was only a "side gig." I quickly realized that having one foot in my own practice, and one foot in my corporate career was not serving anybody well, especially myself and my family. I was only doing a half-ass job and was not able to generate the amount of income (or impact) needed to turn my side-gig into a full-time job, not while still working full-time as a pharmacist, at least. A month or so into trying to balance both, I couldn't tolerate the pain any longer. I had to make a decision and move forward. There are always more decisions to make. Knowing when and how to make them is the most important part of implementing change.

At this point, I was hitting yet another rock bottom. In July 2020, I decided to attend a huge virtual event hosted by the same highly recognized business and life strategist whose tribe I was already a part of. My kids saw me go through a transformational breakthrough, they heard me speak my goals out loud and knew that I was working to find a way to work from home so I would be able to be home with them. This event changed my life. It was there that I gained clarity of what I wanted to do. In large part, this was because I was surrounded by others who were hungry for growth as much as I was. I broke through my fears of failure by physically breaking a board in half! On one side of the board, I wrote "Fear of Failure" and on the other side I wrote, "I am unstoppable, I am Wonder Woman." During this virtual event, I listened as person after person told their stories of passion and drive towards making a real difference in this world and supporting others along the way.

I had finally gained clarity about my calling and got the guts to pursue my purpose to help others rewrite their stories to become the best version of themselves, just like I was doing! This realization came at the perfect time in my life. I finally realized that in order to truly rewrite my story, I had to put two feet into my functional medicine practice and work through the uncomfortable feelings associated with the risk.

Come August 2020, my kids were starting online school again, just like the majority of kids in the nation. Knowing I had no reliable childcare, I made the terrifying decision to take a huge pay cut, and walk away from my full-time job. This was the most stable job I had ever had, as I had been working there for over a decade. Letting go of my job allowed me to focus 100% on my family and in my new practice. I walked away from my 6-figure career and reputation as a leading pharmacist, to step into the space of entrepreneurship. It was a risk but it was also the goal that I had been manifesting all year.

The pandemic made me realize just how quickly our lives can change and how much we can do to change our lives if we have a burning desire to pursue our purpose. Walking away from security and moving forward without the answers totally goes against my life-long training of doing the research before taking action. It was scary, but also so exciting. And it all just felt so right, and there was finally space in my life for me to relax and enjoy time with my family.

After leaving my job, I spent an entire month slowing down and catching up with life. I will never forget the feeling of waking up the following morning and feeling free! I felt like 1,000 pounds of weight was lifted off of my shoulders. I wasn't rushing anywhere, I wasn't hitting the snooze on the alarm over and over. There was nowhere to go. I was finally able to just be present with my family. That morning, I became a full-time mom for the very first time. It actually happened to be a very special day in which I had the privilege of witnessing my son receive his black belt in Tae Kwon Do. I sat back, thinking about how I had been a part-time mom for over a decade and missed out on so many milestones but that was no longer my heartbreaking reality. Witnessing my son earn his black belt was the best feeling this mamma could have ever asked for. We both accomplished something that was scary and took a lot of grit to accomplish. It was hard work, but we did it!

The reason I am sharing all these details is that they each played a key part in my story. We are often told things like, "everything will work out" and "everything happens for a reason." I believe this is true, even though we may not see or understand it at the moment. Remember, my health transformation started in 2015 after hearing my doctor tell me I would have a heart attack within 5 years if I didn't start taking a pill and losing weight. Honestly, if my doctor didn't use those words to "scare" me, I wouldn't have taken my health as seriously as I did. I wouldn't have immediately looked for a better way to take care of my health. I wouldn't have found holistic health. I wouldn't have found my tribe and community who continues to inspire me every single day. Everything really does happen for a reason, and at just the right time in our lives. Painful moments are often the puzzle pieces of life that come together to create a beautiful masterpiece later in life.

If you are experiencing rejection from something you have worked so hard for, consider it to be a redirection towards your next big thing. I have been rejected several times, two of which I will never forget. First, I was rejected from multiple pharmacy schools in California, only to be put on a waitlist with no hope of getting in. Then, I moved all the way to Florida, only to find out that same day that one of the schools in California actually decided to accept me. Frustration and confusion could have set in, but instead, I knew there was a reason I went to school in Florida. If I hadn't made the scary decision to move to Florida, I would never have met some of my best friends. There is a reason I was rejected from a position I applied for within my pharmacy department. If I had started with that position, it would have kept me in the same place for many years instead of stepping into something new – my real purpose. It's no secret that life will suck sometimes. At times, it may seem as though life is unfair, and to be completely honest, sometimes it is. Don't let that distract you from the lessons learned you are meant to learn though and trust the path you are being redirected to. Stay the course, your course, and all really will work out in the end.

When I made the conscious decision to slow down and take the entire month of September off, I began manifesting and visualizing how I would be spending my days, where I would focus my energy, and how I could serve those who need me the most. When I first launched my online practice, I focused on helping women lose weight, detox their bodies, gain energy, and reduce stress. Those were my main pillars of health that I knew for a fact would change their lives. In addition to these pillars, I offered functional-medicine-specific lab testing to take the guesswork out in order to focus on the root cause. I knew there were a lot of women who were struggling and desperately looking for solutions that I could offer.

Part of me kept holding back from going all in and scaling my clinical services up because I found myself having dozens of conversations with other burnt-out pharmacists who were in the exact same shoes as I was. They were also stuck between two worlds, choosing between their career that no longer fulfilled them and their families who needed them. Hearing my colleagues go through the same pain and struggle, I knew I had to provide them with a solution and help them out in a way that nobody else has yet to offer. At this time, I had many tearful conversations with colleagues and other pharmacists who wanted to know how they could also reclaim their lives. Many of these people were moms who were in very similar shoes as I was. They were stressed, overwhelmed, and overworked, while also not making the impact on their patients that they desperately longed for. These conversations made me realize that I needed to invest in my own growth, so I could show up for these women and be able to lead as their mentor as their business coach.

After some time of working 1:1 with clients through my service-based functional medicine practice, I knew that I was still being called to expand my reach beyond working with individual women on a 1:1 basis. The conversations I was having with other clinicians led me to experience a vision of leading other clinicians away from a life riddled with corporate burnout and outlandish expectations to a life of freedom that, I knew first-hand, was possible. After more months of research and business coaching, I accepted the first member into the Functional Medicine Business Academy™ (FMBA) on November 11th, 2020. FMBA was originally a 6-month coaching program but I soon realized that there was a gap in the functional medicine space that I needed to fill. Clinicians are highly educated individuals, and coaching was just the beginning of what they needed to gain the confidence and knowledge in order to open their own practices. This was when I started working with a lawyer to build a credentialed program that was unlike anything else available. Today, the FMBA has become a nationally recognized certification program, offering clinicians the ability to become a Certified Functional Medicine Specialist™.

Around the same time that I launched the FMBA, I also launched the *STORRIE*™ *Podcast* and wrote a best-selling book, *Pivot with Purpose*. All of these decisions took a lot of dedication and commitment, but all along I have been determined to make the impact that I am created to make by helping others to discover their own functional medicine legacies.

Over the last 18 months, the FMBA has gone through many changes. I've known all along that what I am building has to be unique and different. It took me about 6 months of constant research, collaboration, and strategy to add more and more value to FMBA until it was finally ready to be presented as the world's first Functional Medicine Certification Program. I knew how important certification is in the medical world and how important it was to merge clinical mentorship with business mentorship. This will also be a foundation part of my brand, but my vision has expanded since the creation of the FMBA.

Looking back, I realize that I didn't do everything perfectly but I am glad I've been able to learn from my mistakes so that I can help equip others to do things differently. When I first started my business, there were lots of people I took advice from. Some of it was great, but just not for me and my business. Here's the lesson from that: You don't know what you don't know. Not many people have walked the path before me in this industry, so I just pulled as much as I could from the resources and support that was available. I am thankful for everything that I've gone through because now I am able to also pull from my experiences to help serve my clinicians and equip them to be better prepared when they are starting their own practices and begin working with clients. I learned a lot of things the hard way. Nonetheless, I made strides forward with every decision I made. Good and bad decisions have only made the foundation of my business stronger and more able to withstand the challenges to come.

That's the thing with entrepreneurship that not a lot of people talk about– problem-solving. When you become an entrepreneur, you may not realize it but you are signing up to become an expert problem solver. Issues come up each and every day, and it's up to you to figure out the best solution. You won't always get it right on the first try, either. Let me give you an example from my own life: Mid-2021. I got to the point in business where I realized that in order to continue scaling my business and serving more people, I would need to build a team. Up until this point, I had been paying for individual services on a project-by-project basis. It started by hiring my Executive Assistant, Savannah Higgins. She started with me in September 2021 and we were able to start building more of a solid foundation for the FMBA, but still needed more internal support. I went on to hire a business strategist, Zack Line, who specialized in sales to help with an upcoming masterclass in which I would be opening up the academy to welcome new members again. A few months later, I brought on another team member, Danielle Damrell, our Creative Director, who has written the forward for this book. All of this to say, I hired three amazing people to join my team but I soon realized that not everyone would be the right fit for my team. In January 2022, I hired two more people to help with another launch I was having and quickly realized that they were not equipped to do the jobs I had expected them to do. This was a huge learning lesson for me that cost my team and I money, time, and confusion. As I mentioned previously, however, there is a reason for everything that happens in our lives. I learned a valuable lesson from this, and my team rallied around me to ensure we still carried out the launch to the very best of our abilities. We were still able to welcome several clinicians into the tribe, and I was so proud of our team for showing up despite the difficulties that arose. Obviously, I quickly realized that growing a team was no small task. It came with more highs and lows than I ever could have imagined. The biggest lesson I've learned from this experience was to choose your inner circle wisely. Make intentional decisions with whom you decide to let into your team and entrust your business to.

Another valuable lesson I've learned over the course of my entrepreneurship, journey is that I built my business backward. Without realizing what I was doing at the time, I was giving clinicians clinical resources without fully explaining or understanding them myself because I was more focused on teaching the business side of things. Like I said before, you don't know what you don't know, and now I am committed to filling in those gaps for the clinical side of my business.

Through the conversations, coaching, and feedback I have received over the years, we are finally at a pivotal point of combining all that has already been built through the FMBA, with something entirely new. There is a clear need to revolutionize how clinicians are able to practice healthcare, and I am committed to paving the path for them to make the kind of impact we all set out to make when pursuing the field of medicine. I am excited to announce that come April 2022, we will officially be known as *The STORRIE™ Institute*. The reason for this change is simple – Clinicians need a place to go to learn both the clinical side of functional medicine and be equipped with the business skills to build a profitable and successful practice. Unlike other functional medicine certification programs that only focus on clinical skills, The STORRIE™ Institute provides both clinical and entrepreneurial skills. Not only do clinicians get a specialized certification and the opportunity to become a published author, but they also get support from a team and tribe unlike any other. The name "Functional Medicine Business Academy™" was limiting our capacity for impact to only the business side, instead of both clinical and professional development.

My dream is that The *STORRIE*™ institute would also fill a gap for clinicians coming out of university. I see the need for students to have a place to go to combine their education with their passion to help others find real healing. Through this institute, I can help them start their careers creating the kind of impact they are passionate about making. We serve a variety of clinicians with varying credentials including PharmD, MD, DO, DC, NP, PA, PT and RN. With this in mind, students coming out of any number of medical programs would be able to join our tribe and gain credibility and visibility without the years of clinical experience it typically takes before a practitioner can become "successful" in the field of medicine.

The first step of building The STORRIE™ Institute was developing *The STORRIE™ Method.*

The STORRIE™ Method –

S - START WITH YOU
T - TAKE BACK YOUR TIME
O - OPEN OPPORTUNITIES
R - REAL RELATIONSHIPS
R - READY FOR BUSINESS

I - INVEST IN YOUR FUTURE

E - EXPAND YOUR NETWORK

This method was strategically developed to walk clinicians through the process of building a successful practice, from beginning to end. We are creating a foundation for the future of healthcare and practitioners alike. *The STORRIE™ Method* now serves as the foundation of each clinician's journey throughout their time with us. Each step is in place to ensure they have a strategic plan of action to get them started and help them have all the steps to build a sustainable business. This 7-step method is designed to ensure each clinician achieves the life-long results they are in pursuit of! My own experiences caused me to realize that, as clinicians, we function the best when we have structure. As the FMBA tribe grew, I started to realize that not only does my business need structure and a solid foundation, but that's exactly what my tribe of clinicians needed as well. This is precisely what led me towards developing *The STORRIE™ Method* so that clinicians could have a clear understanding of how to launch and scale their own practice.

Another reason we have developed this method is to help clinicians avoid feeling overwhelmed and burnt out. We work hard within the tribe to meet each clinician where they are in their life currently, and develop a plan of action to help them meet their goals. This was another reason I realized I needed to build a team. I could no longer offer each member of our tribe the type of accountability and coaching they required in order to feel well-supported and equipped to take the next step in building their businesses. I had done the work and had grown my tribe of clinicians, but I needed my team to help support my clinicians in the way I no longer had the capacity to.

I recently learned about how there are typically two types of business owners – visionaries and integrators. It is no surprise that I am a visionary.

I have a vision of what I want, but I often don't have the knowledge or expertise to bring my vision to fruition. That's another reason why I need my team. I know for a fact that you can't build a successful business alone. If you have a product-based business, you need customers. If you have a service-based business, you need clients. If your business grows, you need employees. And as I said before, if you're a visionary, you need your integrators at each step of the way. I am so grateful to have found my people who are just as determined as I am to impact the lives of others through the healing power and knowledge of functional medicine. This is the foundation of all that I've done and will continue to do through The *STORRIE™ Institute.*

As we have begun rebranding into The *STORRIE™ Institute,* we are laser-focused on developing leaders in this industry. We are molding and forming the clinical offerings day-by-day to ensure clinicians feel well-equipped to make the lasting impact on their clients' lives that they have set out to make. My personal mission has and will continue to be sharing the good news that *everyone deserves a second chance to rewrite their story and become the best version of themselves.* My professional mission, however, has developed into something much more focused on the impact of functional medicine. Now, I am on a mission to *transform one million lives around the world through functional medicine.* I plan to do this by equipping other clinicians with the tools and resources to use functional medicine as the freshly recognized standard of healthcare. Patients deserve to be heard, valued, and seen. Clinicians deserve to use their knowledge and education to help clients find real healing and live their lives to the fullest. People no longer need to be held back by the symptoms and illnesses that have plagued their lives for far too long. There are real answers out there, and I am determined to help 1 million people find true healing through the impact and practice of the clinicians who come through our program.

Through every pivot and shift in my business, I've had to face the realization that it's okay to change your mind. Your vision might change and develop into something totally different than you had originally thought, and that is entirely ok. As you make decisions and enact changes over the course of your life, you will discover your lane as you go. That's the beautiful thing about life. Even if we have to rewrite our story over and over again, we have the freedom and opportunity to do so each and every day. As for my story, I know that we are just beginning to write the next chapter – The STORRIE™ Institute chapter. There is so much more to come as we are continually building programs that serve people worldwide and will last for generations to come. In this chapter, we are creating the functional medicine revolution.

ABOUT DR. CHRISTINE MANUKYAN

Dr. Christine Manukyan is a Functional Medicine Practitioner, 2x bestselling author and top-ranked STORRIE™ Podcast host. Prior to becoming an entrepreneur, she spent 13 years in Corporate America as a Clinical Pharmacist with various leadership roles. After experiencing her own health transformation with Functional Medicine, losing 100+ lbs and becoming a natural bodybuilding athlete and marathon runner, she found her true calling empowering others to reach their health goals without pharmaceuticals using a holistic lifestyle approach. Dr. Christine has helped more than 300 clients transform their health and rewrite their stories.

Dr. Christine is the founder and CEO of *The STORRIE™ Institute*, the world-leading accountability-based business incubator and functional medicine certification program for clinicians to launch and scale a profitable 6 to 7 figure Functional Medicine practice. She is on a mission to impact 1 million lives around the world with functional medicine.

Dr. Christine is a frequent speaker on holistic lifestyle choices, creating a virtual business, founder and entrepreneur mindset, and creating

multiple income streams. She has spoken in front of audiences num-
bering 15,000+ and has been recognized globally for her entrepreneurial achievement and dedication. Her past publications and magazine
features include FORBES, Yahoo, Disruptors, Authority and BRAINZ
Magazine.

Dr. Christine is leading the **Functional Medicine Revolution** and is
passionate about mentoring burned-out medical professionals struggling
to balance family, career, and their health to take control of their life and
career and create a profitable functional medicine practice.

Dr. Christine believes that everyone deserves a second chance to rewrite their story and become the best version of themselves.

www.drchristinemanukyan.com | drchristine@storrie.co |
IG: @dr.christine.manukyan

Joi our community on Facebook:
Functional Medicine Business Coaching for Clinicians

Chapter 2

FIGHT FOR IT

By: Dr. Beth Bryan, PharmD, CFMS

"If a thing is worth doing, it is worth doing well. If it is worth having, it is worth waiting for. If it is worth attaining, it is worth fighting for. If it is worth experiencing, it is worth putting aside time for."

– OSCAR WILDE

It was a nice spring day in 1993, the location was East Tennessee State University (ETSU), and the class was American History. I was twelve years old and was sitting in a college class. The college professor looked around the room and asked, "Who can tell me the name of the person who made our first American flag?" As he looked for someone to answer his middle school level question, his eyes fixated on me. I had a sinking feeling in my stomach as I thought to myself, "Oh no! Please don't call on me!" As he continued staring at me, he said, "I bet you know the answer." I shook my head nervously side to side, "NO!" Although I did know the answer to his question, I was too bashful to even think about answering. We had learned about Betty Ross the year before when I was in seventh grade during history class. Why on earth was I sitting in a college American History course at twelve years old? No, it wasn't because I was a child prodigy or a genius, though I'd like you to think that. My mother, for some unknown but awesome reason, had allowed me to skip school and spend a couple of nights with my aunt. My aunt is seven years older than me, and was attending ETSU for her freshman year. My aunt picked me up and took me grocery shopping and then we went to her dorm room where I spent the night. The next day, we woke up early and attended all her classes together. A few minutes after the professor asked me the question, my aunt winked at me and handed me some of her peanut M&Ms to snack on. How cool it was to get to eat candy during class? I had even more fun playing racquetball with her later in the day during her physical education class. I remember the tiny door, the odd-looking room, and the one-on-one game I played against my aunt. I can't remember who won the game, but this early college experience had a lasting impression on me. I felt so grown up and I didn't know how I would do it, but I knew that someday, somehow, I had to go to college. I knew there was something more out there than scraping by from day to day. I had a hunger for knowledge, I was like a sponge, taking in every bit of new information that came my way. Though no one in my family ended up graduating from college, just knowing there was an opportunity like that gave me enough vision to know that if I worked hard, I could have an amazing life. I decided then I was going to fight for it, and that is exactly what I did. I fought hard by working my way through undergrad while also working outside jobs to provide for myself. I was extremely bashful and knew I was going to have to step outside my comfort zone to achieve my college dream. I was scared, but I did it anyway.

Growing up, I remember many times when we didn't know where our next meal would come from or how we would afford my sister's life-saving medication. I remember looking for loose change in the couch cushions and walking to the store with my family for a snack and drink. My young parents lived paycheck to paycheck, doing the best they could with their young family. By the time my father was 22 and my mom 20, they had 3 bouncing babies to raise. My father served in the U.S. Navy for eight years, providing financially for us while my mom took care of us three kids. I can remember the last time my father came home from his service. I was supposed to be in bed, but when I heard his voice, I couldn't resist the temptation to run to him. The risk paid off because I got some rare alone time with him and was able to stay up a little later before returning to bed. Not long after my father returned home, my 4-year-old sister Nikki had a life changing emergency. My mom took her to the emergency room (ER) because she was turning blue and struggling to breathe. The ER kept telling my mother that Nikki was fine and sent her home. Mom went back to the ER for the third time in a row begging for someone to listen to the fact that she was turning blue, and something was very wrong. My mom was told that she was being an overprotective mother and to just take her home. Eventually, my mom refused to leave and told them she wasn't going anywhere until her daughter was properly assessed. An ER physician intervened, realizing that my sister's lungs had collapsed and immediately had her airlifted to The University of Tennessee Children's Hospital which was two hours from our home. They didn't expect her to survive the flight, but she did! After some time in the intensive care unit (ICU), she started making improvements. She has trouble with her lungs to this day, but we are so grateful that my mom fought for her! My mother saved my little sister's life because she was willing to fight for her and refused to be turned away from care. Despite being insulted and sent away three times, my mother kept pushing and fighting until someone listened and acted to save her child.

Seeing my mother care for my sister helped me learn basic patient care skills and how to have empathy for others. She taught me to fight for the underdog in life. She helped me understand what it meant for a patient not to be heard, and how to continue asking questions until I received a real answer. I began working in an independent pharmacy when I was 17 years old. I would work after school because I was in the early release program. I would leave high school at lunch and take care of cashier duties until the pharmacy closed. I started learning technician skills and decided during my senior year that I wanted to become a pharmacy technician. It was hilarious that I chose this route because my career assessment in high school said I would be best equipped to become a professional football player, all 100 pounds of my nonathletic self. Since football wasn't a good fit for me, I opted for pharmacy and I worked as a pharmacy technician, and then later a pharmacy intern until I finished my time at pharmacy school. My love for community pharmacy came from enjoying the challenges that came up daily and figuring out how to solve almost any problem that came my way. Focusing on the patients, their needs, their frustrations, their joys, and the interactions that I get to have with them is where my heart finds the most fulfillment. I can advocate for the patients that are not being heard by their healthcare providers, insurances, and sometimes even their own caregivers. Most people go into healthcare to help their patients, but many times I see patients needs are left unmet. It's not usually because the healthcare providers don't want to help them, it's because the structure of our current medical system does not allow for whole patient care to be the priority. It is my mission to fill that gap and find real solutions for them.

I began my career as a pharmacist, working for a Walmart pharmacy in my hometown. Although I really enjoyed my development as a pharmacist and leader, I longed to be back in independent pharmacy. I simply missed the personal relationships with my patients and the ability to extend extra help and assistance to them. After working for a Walmart pharmacy for four and a half years, I left my pharmacy management role to purchase an independent pharmacy just two miles from where I attended middle school. This was the same middle school where I skipped school to attend college with my aunt back in 1993. When you hear that life can come full circle, please believe that it certainly can because that is exactly what happened to me. I ended up buying the pharmacy from the same pharmacist I worked for when I first graduated from high school and was attending the local community college in pursuit of my pharmacy technician certification.

Never in my wildest dreams did I think I would become a female leader in my community. I am now a business owner and an entrepreneur because this what my hard work and dedication has led me towards becoming. No one would have believed what my future has had in store, especially considering how reserved I was as a child. To everyone's surprise, this is in fact, what my fighting spirit has led to. Looking back, I didn't stand much of a chance with the obstacles that I had overcome in life. I had no way to pay for college, but I made a way by budgeting my money and paying everything off along the way. I always had a desire to work and dreamed of being successful, but never dreamed of pharmacy ownership or leading my employees in the ways that I have. One of my technicians was awarded a national award, *Technician of the Year*, in October 2021.

It is my goal to encourage my employees to practice at the top of their licenses and help move the field of community pharmacy forward. I have a dream for us as a profession, to do more for our patients. I know we can do more, I see the difference we make in patient lives every day, and it is incredibly underestimated. As the years have passed in my career, I couldn't help but notice how much community pharmacies do within communities and patients nationwide. My pharmacy in particular is actually the only existing form of healthcare in town. There are no doctors' offices or clinics, just me and my pharmacy team to help with our community's healthcare needs. This has led me to practice pharmacy in a way that isn't very typical within many community pharmacies. We were the first immunizing pharmacy, even amongst neighboring towns. We were the first to offer point-of-care testing such as flu and strep tests, so our community would have the option to get timely diagnosis and treatment. In 2020, we were the first independent pharmacy in the nation to offer COVID-19 testing because we felt the need to help our community, and we learned very quickly that it was truly a massive need. I never felt the push to be first in these services but I felt the need to offer these services since my community already has limited options for seeking healthcare. Fulfilling these needs has resulted in pushing our practice to all-new levels of services. Right now, the times are incredibly difficult for community pharmacies with massive direct and indirect remuneration (DIR) fees as well as below cost reimbursements. I have put up an incredible fight to remain here in order for my patients to have access to quality healthcare. It is just another thing that I have learned to fight for, and I will continue to keep pharmacy in this rural community as long as I am able.

During my twenty-year career in providing care in community pharmacy, I have noticed that there seems to be a revolving door most patients cycle through. I started noticing that they never truly get better, at least not from the chronic conditions that affect them. It's as though their symptoms are treated instead of their actual condition, or worse, they are given another prescription to deal with side effects from another medication. COVID-19 has made it even harder for patients to receive proper healthcare, and I see more needs going unmet than ever before. I began a research journey to find a better way to treat illness, especially the chronic conditions that I see every day. As a pharmacist, I do believe in the power of conventional medication, but I also believe that not all situations require another medication to be prescribed. Hence, the revolving door of "a pill for every ill", yet no real resolve of disease.

My research led me to functional medicine and how it addresses the root cause of health conditions rather than symptomatic treatment. Although I knew becoming a functional medication specialist would require a ton of work and research, I decided that it would be worth it. It had to be worth fighting for a better way for my patients to not only be heard, but to actually start getting better. I understand what it is like to be an unheard patient myself, as I have been trying to get to the root cause of my symptoms and autoimmune deficiencies since I was a teenager. I went to multiple specialists and spent thousands of dollars, just to be misdiagnosed, disregarded, and handed a prescription that truly, just made me feel worse. A twenty-year journey that led me to absolutely zero answers other than the ones I have discovered through my own research. My young daughter has already experienced this revolving loop of side effects, food allergies, and never reaching the root cause of her symptoms either.

The good news is, this revolving door can be stopped! It only takes one provider giving a patient the time and listening to what is actually going in order to start putting the pieces together. I decided that after years of watching family members struggle with autoimmune diseases, it was up to me to learn how to reverse and avoid them not only for myself, but also for my kids and any future generations to come. I have done the research and I have learned that there is a better way for patients suffering chronic symptoms and diseases. Diseases and conditions can be reversed and even prevented to begin with. How we do this through a practice is called functional medicine.

The first time I heard about functional medicine was at a pharmacy conference in 2019. I ended up in a class in which the speaker was talking about functional medicine and how it can help patients. She talked about a young woman that became addicted to opioids at the age of 19 after she was prescribed hydrocodone for her wisdom teeth extraction. This young woman tried everything she could to fight the addiction, but her cravings for the drugs remained prominent. She kept falling back into her drug addiction, no matter how much she wanted to be free from it. She was treated by a functional medicine specialist that discovered this young lady had a severe vitamin deficiency. They worked on improving the deficiency, and in time the lady realized that her cravings for opioids were diminishing. This young lady not only beat drug addiction, but she also went on to college and became a working and successful member of society. She became a lawyer.

I was so impressed and inspired by this story that I had to know more about functional medicine. Can correcting a simple vitamin deficiency really change a life or even save a life? Could this knowledge about a person's body have saved my sister-in-law, who had recently passed away as a result of a drug addiction? Maybe if someone had looked deeper look into her body, vitamin levels, and mental health, her life could have been saved. Maybe if someone could have treated her with kindness and humanity and actually looked at underlying reasons for her drug addiction, she would have stood a chance at life instead of succumbing to her addiction. Perhaps there could have been a road to recovery if she had been accessed to find a root cause of her addiction. She died at 31 years of age, leaving behind two beautiful children and a family that dreamed of a life with her.

I have since read articles that show there is a link between vitamin D deficiency and opioid addiction. I don't know if vitamin D deficiency was the young lady's vitamin deficiency from the story earlier, but I am curious to find out more as more research is done in opioid addiction and vitamin deficiencies. I believe if my sister-in-law knew that taking a deeper dive into her health from within could have helped with her addiction, she would have fought for her life. Let's dig into functional medicine a bit more and so I can expand on why this is such a powerful form of medicine.

Functional medicine is a scientific, integrative, patient-centered, individualized, and systems-oriented approach to finding the root cause of disease. Functional medicine also focuses on maximizing health and nutrition so the body can function in the best way possible. All aspects of nutrition, lifestyle, metabolism, hormones, and genetics can be considered for an individualized approach. Every patient is treated individually and wholly, instead of the typical cookie cutter approach known through conventional medicine. The more a person knows about their body, the more they can maximize their potential health.

Another difference between functional medicine and conventional medicine is that in functional medicine, we use a preventative approach rather than a reactive approach. That means we try to prevent the onset of a disease rather than waiting until a disease manifests. Another difference that is important to note in conventional medicine, is that once a patient has a disease, they will most likely keep that disease for life. Functional medicine has proven that many diseases can be reversed with proper nutrition and lifestyle changes. Even in conventional medicine, we know and acknowledge that diabetes can be prevented and even reversed with lifestyle changes and exercise. Functional medicine goes above just lifestyle changes, although it is a large part of healing. We also investigate other components of disease such as genetic, nutrigenomics, hormonal, and laboratory values to create an individualized treatment plan. The fact that we can, in fact, prevent disease is exciting as not only a healthcare provider, but also as a patient.

As I mentioned earlier, most of my family from my mother's side suffers from autoimmune diseases, mostly gastrointestinal, rheumatic, as well as connective tissue diseases. I have already been fighting my own connective tissue disease, that has resulted in multiple surgeries and gastro complications. I am on a healing journey and hope to eliminate my disease completely. My daughter has already suffered gastrointestinal issues, headaches, and food allergies. Her initial symptom was severe pain that led to an urgent care visit and then the ER. Her bowels were completely packed and shut down to the point that nothing we were giving her was making them work. Her pediatrician discovered that she had a temporary paralysis of her intestines also known as "ileus" which is a rare condition for children to experience. During this time, it was also discovered that she had a gluten allergy. She was put on a liquid diet for 10 days, which was extremely difficult for her as she was only 8 years old and she already felt terrible. She is now 10 and still having some symptoms, although they have significantly improved. Through specialized testing, I was able to administer a food sensitivity test and discovered that she has a high sensitivity to dairy and eggs. We have started an elimination diet and probiotics to heal her gut and eliminate her symptoms altogether. She is getting stronger and feeling better, which makes me and her both very happy. I have learned the importance of proper nutrition through diet and exercise to create a strong immune system and body. The knowledge we have learned from our labs, my research, and health protocols are life changing. Now, I help others achieve optimal strength and health in body, mind, and spirit. We do not have to settle for a debilitating, low energy, and non-functioning life because there really is a better way to live!

Reversing a disease is a journey and I am so happy I have the honor of helping people get on a path towards healing so that they can feel their best physically, emotionally, and mentally. I named my functional medicine practice *Reverse Functional Medicine*™ because I have witnessed the power of reversing diseases firsthand. I know for a long time people have thought they had to live with their diseases for life, but that is not the case. The freedom and chance to live a life free of disease is life changing, and it is worth the work that becomes effortless in time.

Currently, I help people with autoimmune diseases take control of their lives and their well-being. I offer both group sessions and one-on-one sessions to clients wanting to put their autoimmune diseases into remission, reduce their symptoms, and improve their overall quality of life. I also offer an autoimmune immersion or detox program to fast track healing by removing toxins and getting the body ready for positive changes. My patients experienced positive results within just the first week. The detox program also helps get their bodies ready for healing and the absorbing of nutrients that their bodies may be in need of. I often order labs to help the patients learn more about their bodies nutrient levels, food sensitivities, and the condition of their gut. We use the test results to plan out an individual plan of action to decrease inflammation, gastrointestinal symptoms, and improve gut health energy. It is very rewarding to give my patients the experience where a healthcare provider listens to them and helps guide them in healing and eliminating the symptoms that have been plaguing their lives for far too long. I will never stop fighting for those voices that aren't heard and providing resources for patients to find relief.

I want to leave you with some questions about your own health and life that I would like you to ponder. What in your life are you willing to fight for it? Is there anything holding you back? Is it awareness, knowledge, time, or money? What solutions can you come up with to achieve your goals and desires? Are you getting your health where you need it to be? And lastly, what have you spent financially to improve your health and how did you get the results you desired? I ask this question because in my own journey, I have spent thousands and thousands of dollars trying to get better just to end up in the revolving "pill for every ill" door. I will continue to learn as much as I can about my body, nutrition, mind, and environment. I will make any necessary changes so I can live the best, healthiest, and most energetic life possible. I want to feel good and enjoy movement, and I am most certainly willing to fight for it. I encourage you to get out of the revolving door, learn more about your body, and fight to feel like yourself again because you are worth fighting for!

ABOUT DR. BETH BRYAN

Dr. Beth Bryan is a Certified Functional Medicine Specialist™ from The STORRIE™ Institute, Nationally Certified Lifestyle Coach, Diabetes Care & Education Specialist, Pharmacy Entrepreneur, and Pharmacy Owner. Dr. Beth has over two decades of pharmacy experience and has been a pharmacist for thirteen years. She enjoys problem-solving, learning new strategies, and direct patient care. Her passions for patient care are fueled by the nuances, misunderstandings, and sometimes lack of care in the current healthcare systems.

Dr. Beth helps people with autoimmune diseases take control of their lives and their well-being. She offers both group sessions and one-on-one sessions to clients wanting to put their autoimmune diseases into remission, reduce their symptoms, and improve their overall quality of life. Most patients experienced positive results within just the first week. The detox program also helps get their bodies ready for healing and the absorbing of nutrients that their bodies may be in need of.

Dr. Beth enjoys spending time with her family, including her two children and husband of twenty years. She enjoys almost any exercise including running, biking, hiking, and most recently karate with her kids. Getting away for mini-vacations with her family to reset and refill her cup so that she can continue serving and helping others.

Dr. Beth is eager to continue building on her knowledge and foundations in medicine, nutrition, and lifestyles. Her hunger for knowledge and determination to turn information into action is how she equips patients to reach their own health goals. She has learned the importance of proper nutrition through diet and exercise to create a strong body. The knowledge she has learned from labs, research, and health protocols is life-changing. Now, she helps others achieve optimal strength and health in body, mind, and spirit. Dr. Beth Bryan is on a mission to help others not settle for a debilitating, low energy, and non-functioning life because she knows the path towards a better way to live!

www.surgoinsvillepharmacy.com | info@drbethbryan.com | Facebook: /drbethbryan | Instagram: @drbethbryan | LinkedIn: /drbethbryan

Chapter 3

EMBRACE YOUR INHERENT POWER TO HEAL

By: Charyse Williams, RN and Holistic Health Coach

"We don't have a healthcare problem, we have a self-care problem"
– Dr. Michael Beckwith

I remember like it was yesterday, I was standing in front of room 22 in the Surgical Intensive Care Unit and I had this thought, "We are doing something wrong." By "we", I was referring to society as a whole and the current healthcare model, specifically. When I became a nurse in 1996, the majority of the patients I was seeing in the Intensive Care Units (ICU) were 60 to 100 years old. Fast-forward about 8 years and the majority of the patients I was seeing in ICU were much younger- 30, 40, and 50-year-olds. I remember thinking, "How are we getting sicker, younger?" It was at that moment that I became very disenchanted with the current healthcare model.

I became a nurse because I wanted to help people get better. I wanted to educate people on how to take better care of themselves so that they would not have to come back to the ICU. Unfortunately, what ended up happening was that I became a professional drug dealer. I spent my entire shift titrating drips and educating my patients on what their medications were and why I was giving it to them. I was not able to talk to them about how they could stay out of the hospital and how they could improve their health to the point that they would not need to take medications at all. It was at that time that I transitioned from critical care nursing to Nursing Informatics. I realized that being an ICU nurse was no longer in alignment with who I was becoming as a person, and who I wanted to be as a practitioner.

Shortly after beginning to work in Nursing Informatics, I decided to start my own project management and training consulting business, where I would either travel the country teaching nurses and doctors how to use different EMRs (electronic medical records) or manage the entire process. This was so fulfilling, however, it required that I leave my husband and two sons for long lengths of time. I went from working 12-hour night shifts in ICU to traveling from state to state for sometimes months at a time. Every week I was in a different part of the country and was living out of a suitcase. Oftentimes, I was too tired to go grocery shopping or eat out at a restaurant. Most of the time, I would simply leave the hospital site that I was working at, grab food from a fast-food restaurant, and sit on my bed in my hotel room. It was not uncommon to eat Chick-Fil-A french fries and drink lemonade while burning the midnight oil, continuing to work through the night. Sometimes I would work 16 to 18 hours. Needless to say, I was exhausted ALL the time.

My fatigue was at an all-time high. My knee pain was excruciating because of all the excess weight that I had been carrying around for so many years. And obviously, my sleep pattern was completely off. It was almost non-existent. The weight, the stress, the inflammation, the pain, the exhaustion, this is what I was left with. I, like so many high-achieving and high-performing women, was absolutely crushing it in my career, but to the detriment of my own health. I knew there had to be a better way to live, and I knew that I absolutely needed to reclaim my health. I thought about weight loss surgery but ultimately decided it was not for me because, at the end of the day, it did not get to the root of the problem. I also knew that I did not want to continue taking medications for the rest of my life.

You see, I tried the medication route. I had taken different medications for my migraines, and each of them left me feeling like I had a hangover the next day. I would always feel "off." I would go to my doctor and tell them that I didn't like the way I felt when I took my migraine meds. Their answer was always to simply switch my prescription. They never once asked me if I was under a lot of stress. They never asked if I was sleeping or about what I was eating. That was never part of the conversation. The only thing that was said consistently was, "Let's just change your medication."

I came to the realization that much like a bank, my health was really a balance of withdrawals and deposits. For many years, I had taken out so many withdrawals with very few deposits, and now my health account was overdrawn. The decades of working 12-hour night shifts, coupled with 16 to 18-hour shifts while traveling the country with my consulting business, had taken its toll. From the outside, I did not appear to be "sick", but clearly, something was wrong.

I had gone the traditional route of taking medications for the migraines, for the knee pain, for weight loss, and for energy only to be let down time and time again. They were just band-aids to help me "get by" and continue with all of the many things on my to-do list but they never got to the root cause. They weren't designed to. I knew intuitively that there had to be a different way, a better way! That's when I decided it was time to dive into alternative healing modalities. The first place I started was with my food choices. I was intuitively led to a book called *The pH Miracle* by Dr. Joseph Young. It talked all about how we could use food as medicine and that by adopting a primarily whole food plant-based alkaline diet we could reverse most, if not all disease. I was fascinated.

And so it began. I immediately shifted the way that I was eating. I started eating foods that were as close to nature as possible, mostly fresh fruits and vegetables, nuts, seeds, and sprouted grains. The weight just started falling off! I released 80 pounds within about 8 months. My energy came back! The knee pain was gone! The migraines went from twice a week to once every 3-4 months! Then, I started learning more about other natural healing modalities, such as the power of medicinal herbs and how therapeutic essential oils could help support my body as it was healing. I was also introduced to breathwork and the art of meditation by my good friend Jo Anne. I started practicing all of these different modalities and found that not only was I keeping the weight off, but I was managing my stress so much better. I was happier, more energetic, and I finally felt like the true me! I remember thinking, "Why don't more people know about this?" I decided to make it my mission to educate as many people as I could. I became certified as a Holistic Health Coach and a Living on Live Food educator because I knew that in order to continue the path I was on, I would need to learn a different way of caring for myself and others.

People started asking in amazement, "Charyse, what are you doing?" I started sharing what I was doing with anyone who would listen. I got so much joy and fulfillment educating people on all of these different natural modalities. I knew I could teach them how to support their bodies and bring about true healing, all while experiencing incredible results along the way.

You see, the body is always striving for homeostasis or balance. Always. It wants to be healthy and whole. It was designed that way. However, we play an integral role in whether we allow it to do its job. How, you may ask? One way is by the food choices that we make. Unfortunately, we've been misguided about what food *really* is. Think about all of the items that are in your pantry right now. If your pantry is anything like mine was, it's filled with incredibly over-processed food, toxic food. That's how our bodies view it, at least, and it stores it as fat! Secondly, I don't believe we were ever really educated about the toxicity of the products that we put on our bodies like lotions, perfumes/colognes, or even about the products we use to clean our homes from our kitchen to our laundry room. I know I wasn't. Many of those things are hormone disruptors and have a negative impact on our overall health. Thirdly, by mind -body coherence. Mind-body coherence is when our brain (thoughts and decisions) work hand-in-hand with our heart (emotions) and body (actions we take). It is a state of unity between our mind, body, and spirit/soul. When we address a problem or symptom with one of the three, we get limited and short-term results. What is necessary for limitless health and lasting results is to take a holistic and natural approach.

So, what is Holistic health? Holistic health is about considering yourself as a whole person. You are not just a disease. When you understand and emphasize the connections between mind, body, and soul, you will experience a life you may have never thought was possible. Instead of asking what prescriptions can be taken to mask the symptoms you're experiencing, holistic health asks the question, "What non-prescription/ natural options can be used to solve this problem?" Holistic health is all about how the individual can be supported so that the body retains or regains the ability to heal itself, instead of giving away the reins of health to something outside of us, like a pharmaceutical drug. Our bodies have intuitive natural wisdom that knows how to heal itself when given the proper tools like a whole-food, plant-based diet, proper sleep, adequate hydration, fresh air, and a calm mind.

It all boils down to understanding how the food we eat, the thoughts we think, the words we speak, the things we put on our body, our household environment, and even work environments have a profound effect on your body. Don't get me wrong, I am a huge proponent of prescription medication in acute situations. Let's face it, if I have a traumatic injury, please don't feed me a smoothie and tell me to meditate. By all means, please rush me into the operating room with the best trauma surgeon you have. But for everyday maintenance and as a daily practice, these are the things that we can do to keep ourselves healthy and whole and not have to suffer from the types of chronic diseases that we see which, by and large, are lifestyle diseases. Lifestyle diseases, such as type 2 diabetes, hypertension (high blood pressure), and chronic fatigue are completely reversible with adjustments in our daily choices.

An example of this comes from a conversation I had with a good friend just last year. I remember I called my friend, a 50-year-old African-American male, and I asked him how he was doing. He said, "I'm fine. I just left the doctor's office." I asked if everything was ok, and he shared that his blood pressure was elevated and that his doctor put him on medication for it. I asked him if his blood pressure was normally elevated. He said no, and I then asked him if the doctor offered any suggestions on how to naturally decrease his blood pressure before prescribing him an anti-hypertensive. He, to no surprise, replied no. I asked him how long the doctor thought he would have to take the medicine. He said he didn't know and that he may have to take it forever. I then shared with him that there are natural ways to decrease his blood pressure. He said, "Oh, I didn't know that. I thought I was just getting old." How many of us think that we're just getting old and that it's natural for our bodies to fall apart or stop working optimally as we get older? That simply does not have to be the case.

Another personal example I have was from 2021 when I got extremely sick from Covid-19 and had to be hospitalized for eight days. While I am beyond grateful for the team that took care of me, I was so disturbed by the food choices that the hospital had to offer. I found it extremely difficult to even find unprocessed food choices on the menu. The majority of the options were ultra-processed, refined carbs. I could not wait to get out of the hospital for obvious reasons, but one of the main reasons was so I could have access to real, healthy, unadulterated food. Not grilled cheese and a salad with lettuce that was barely green. How can the body heal itself apart from proper nutrition?

I found it so fascinating that during the pandemic I heard very little talk on mainstream media about how to naturally fortify our immune system. No one was mentioning how food affects our health. I wasn't hearing how stress weakens the immune system, and no one was talking about how processed sugar makes us more susceptible to illness. What *was* being said was that if you have chronic illnesses such as high blood pressure, diabetes, or even obesity, you are more likely to have severe COVID-19 symptoms. It was almost as if they were shaming people for having a pre-existing condition yet no one was mentioning how to decrease those comorbidities. I was so frustrated. Not only that, but no one was talking about how improving our gut health would help to strengthen our immune system or that natural supplements, herbs, and foods could help fortify our bodies against this virus. Chronic illness is a pandemic that no one is addressing, but we have studies, research, and resources that could completely end these diseases.

As you can probably tell by now, I am very passionate about helping reverse chronic disease and address "common" (but, really, abnormal)

symptoms that people find themselves experiencing. Our bodies are always communicating to us but we have become so disconnected from our
true selves that we don't know how to interpret what our body is saying.
For instance, when we have a headache, our body is not saying that it is
deficient in acetaminophen (Tylenol). It is communicating that something is "off." Perhaps our blood sugar is low and we need to eat. Perhaps
we are sleep-deprived and we need to rest. Perhaps we are stressed and our
body is communicating with us that we need a time-out. Simply put, we
need to focus on more self-care. I don't think that we have a healthcare
problem, per se. What we really have is a self-care problem. I am guilty
of it myself. Of doing all the things to stay "busy" and putting my health
on the back burner, ignoring the vague symptoms that were trying to
communicate to me that I needed to do something different.

Much of the time, chronic illness is because of poor lifestyle routines
such as eating too much sugar, processed foods, and unhealthy fats often
combined with poor sleep habits and unaddressed high levels of stress.
What I have found from working with high-achieving women is that by
making adjustments in their everyday routines, it allows their bodies to
rebalance itself. If nothing else, the body requires real food. I always say
that if it has an ingredient list on it, then it is processed. Bananas don't
have an ingredient list. Spinach also does not have a list of ingredients.
Once we get back to eating an abundance of foods that do not have a list
of ingredients, our bodies miraculously start to balance and heal themselves. Once we start improving our quality and quantity of sleep, our
body starts recalibrating itself and is able to do what it is designed to do.
Our bodies are created to repair, renew, and restore themselves. Once we
focus on moving our bodies out of a stressed state (which also contributes
to inflammation and will prevent our body from releasing weight) our
adrenals can stop working overtime to produce cortisol, a stress hormone,

and our bodies can start releasing other hormones to stay balanced such as melatonin or serotonin. We all have our own natural pharmacy built within us. Our body is able to provide the perfect chemistry, naturally, but we have to learn how to access those hormones through the decisions we make each and every day.

I have another story for you about one of my clients. This one is about a 65-year-old woman in a leadership position within the medical field. She has had type 2 diabetes and high blood pressure for over 40 years. When we started working together, I immediately helped her adjust the types of foods she was eating, as well as incorporating methods to help her decrease stress. She was like so many. She was even like me at certain times in my career. She was constantly working to get everything done for everyone and not eating at all or eating on the run and burning the midnight oil, day after day. I recommended she change her diet to a primarily whole food plant-based diet, I educated her on particular therapeutic essential oils that would help improve her quality and quantity of sleep and introduced her to meditation and breathwork which helped to decrease her stress levels due to her demanding job. Within the first six weeks of us working together, her Hemoglobin A1C decreased from 11 to 9 and is now 6.0 (normal Hemoglobin A1C is below 5.7). She is well on her way to kicking diabetes to the curb! We have also been able to decrease her blood pressure to the point that her cardiologist decreased her blood pressure medication by half. Her blood pressure has begun to regulate itself naturally.

This woman said she thought reclaiming her health after 40 years would be hard. But when I asked how she felt after working together for about 4 months, she used the words "excited" and "empowered." She said she was confident she was finally on the right path. At a recent doctor's appointment, her doctor said, "I don't know what you're doing, but whatever it is, keep doing it." She told him she was taking a holistic approach to reclaiming her own health. This is the power of equipping your body to heal itself.

Another example from a client of mine is a 50-year-old African American female educator. She has suffered with extreme allergies to the point where she had to take allergy medicine every single day in order to function. Her symptoms were puffy, watery eyes, sneezing, postnasal drip, and congestion. We focused first on optimizing her gut health by changing what she was eating and by incorporating essential oils, probiotics, digestive enzymes, and swapping out some of her household cleaning items. Within 30 days, she was able to stop using her daily allergy medication. This is another powerful example of the healing possible through simple, holistic lifestyle changes.

For the past 7 years, I have been educating and coaching high-achieving women on how to support their bodies and heal themselves naturally. I often share about reversing lifelong disease, eliminating medications, and overcoming health challenges that have held them back from being fully confident and living like the powerhouses they are already. We take a look inside by using my proprietary system, *The Feel Better Faster Formula™- A Holistic Approach.* It excites me to no end when I am educating people on how to reconnect with their bodies and to understand what their bodies really need and educate them on how to properly take care of themselves— mind, body, and soul. My work has been instrumental in helping them to reverse chronic diseases and shifting their long-term health trajectory to one of whole-life wellness. I always share with my clients that they are their own healers, not me. I am simply a conduit and an educator. A healer is not someone we go to for healing. A healer is someone who ignites the ability you have within you, to heal yourself.

A holistic approach to healing, in my opinion, is one of the most effective solutions to truly changing our broken model of healthcare as we know it. Dr. Michael Beckwith says, "We don't have a healthcare model, we have a sick care model." The definition of insanity is doing the same thing over and over again and expecting a different result. The evidence is in front of our very eyes, and we must accept the fact that our system may be broken when it comes to long-term healing and getting to the root causes of the majority of diseases and illnesses. Healing is possible and at this point, we have all had someone in our family affected by cancer, hypertension, diabetes, or an autoimmune disease. Why wouldn't we do everything possible to bring real healing to ourselves and those we love? Maya Angelou said, "When we know better, we do better." We are now becoming more aware as a society and as healthcare professionals, and now we do know better. I believe that we have a duty to educate and empower our communities to own our power and begin to heal first ourselves, then our families, followed by our community which will ultimately heal the world.

ABOUT CHARYSE WILLIAMS

Charyse is a Registered Nurse (RN), Holistic Health Coach, Neu-ro-Transformational Coach, Bestselling Author, Living on Live Food Educator, wife to her high school sweetheart, and mom of 2 wonderful young men. Her expertise has been featured on Beyond the Red Tent, The Peaceful Planet Foundation, numerous podcasts, and as a virtual summit speaker. Charyse is revolutionizing the healthcare industry as a thought leader with her mind, body, and soul approach.

Charyse is the founder and CEO of Green and Gorjus where she teaches high-achieving women how to heal themselves naturally, reverse lifelong disease, eliminate medications, and overcome health challenges that have held them back from being fully confident and living like the powerhouses they are! Her *Feel Better Faster Formula - The Holistic Approach* is the exact formula she used to personally shed 80 pounds, reverse chronic fatigue and eradicate her migraines.

Charyse is passionate about helping women who are seeking alternatives to Western Medicine, identify the root cause of their health challenges, and take a holistic approach that includes using food as medicine, therapeutic essential oils, medicinal herbs, breathwork, meditation, and cultivating a mindset that is in alignment with their health & wellness goals, working WITH their bodies instead of against it. For Charyse, it is all about the mind, body, and soul connection!

www.charysewilliams.com | charysew@greenandgorjus.com | Facebook: @charysew | Instagram: @charysewilliams

Chapter 4

CREATING BALANCE FROM WITHIN

By: Dr. Deepa Pattani, PharmD, RPh, CFMS

"Nature is our biggest teacher. The symptoms that we experience are nature's way of telling us that something is off."

— Dr. Deepa Pattani

Hello! My name is Deepa and I grew up in Mumbai, India until the age of 13 when my family and I immigrated to the United States. Growing up in India meant survival. As a kid, I had experienced a weak gut, weak immune system, malaria, parasites in my stomach, and pneumonia, just to name a few. Vacation or trips outside the hometown meant spending time in lots of restrooms, being nauseous and vomiting. My mom would often be coming up with natural remedies to keep me out of the hospital. This is unfortunately how I remember spending most of our family vacations. We spent many days at the doctor's offices and our particular doctor was very interesting, she knew our entire family and she knew all our complications and diseases. She always tried to steer us towards natural remedies first and then prescribed something at the very end if all else failed. She even had a compounder in the office who would put the medications together and explain to us how to take them before we left the office. This is actually where my love for medicine started. I loved that the compounder was the only one who could understand the doctor's scribbles and made sure we understood the role of each medicine as well as how to properly take it. While my parents talked to the doctor, I would be in the back asking hundreds of questions to the compounder, and little did I know at the time that I would eventually grow up to be a pharmacist.

In May 1998, my journey brought me to New Jersey, where I started high school. I graduated top 1% of my class and got accepted to the accelerated 6-year Doctor of Pharmacy program at Rutgers University. In 2004, at the age of 23, I graduated with a doctorate in pharmacy. This is where I learned everything I know about western medicine and pharmaceuticals. I was excited to take on the world and to help my patients live their best lives. I thought that I would counsel them and have an impact that would drastically enhance their lives. Seems logical right? Unfortunately, this was not my experience at all. I was buried in corporate politics, verifying and filling 400+ prescriptions a day, on my feet for 14 hours a day, and I had an additional 2 hours of travel to and from work each day. There were no bathroom or meal breaks and by the time I got home, I would fall on my bed and sleep before my food could even heat up in the microwave. This went on for about 13 months and my health quickly deteriorated.

I was eating unhealthy, processed, ready-to-eat foods while not exercising and not getting restful sleep. One Monday morning at work, 20 minutes into my shift, I collapsed with tremendous pain in my stomach and rushed off to the hospital in an emergency. When I told my manager I needed to leave, his initial response was, "Could you just hold on for 2 more hours?" He wanted to find someone else to run the pharmacy before I left. I knew at that moment that, my health was my biggest asset, and I could easily be replaced in as little as 2 hours by my employers. The biggest treasure we have is our health and our loved ones. The result from my emergency room visit was that I was diagnosed with a stress ulcer and sent home with a prescription for Protonix.

Being of Asian descent, I grew up hearing all about ayurveda, homeopathic medicine, chinese medicine, acupressure, acupuncture, etc. I had many personal experiences with these practices because natural remedies are what my parents used on us when we were sick. I noticed, however, I didn't have any professional experience using natural medicines though because all my training was in western medicine and symptom treatment. This treatment for the ulcer was a different experience than my previous experiences as a kid. When I was young, my doctor always tried to look for the root causes of illnesses and symptoms. There was no such attempt here, though, and I was experiencing what being a "patient" in America really meant. I was at a loss and I had no idea why I had the stress ulcer. I had no idea how I could prevent it in the future and was only given a pill and had to take it for 6 weeks with no further explanation. I didn't like this feeling of not being in control, of being confused, and not having answers. On my path, there were several instances of when I succumbed to western ways of treatment and, in contrast, also instances when I took to the holistic ways of healing. The distinction was crucial to my life path.

When I was a young girl getting sick on vacations, it was the change in environment and water supply that would get me sick. My immune system was weak and couldn't fight off anything foreign that entered my body. Looking back, I can tell that my weakened immune system was a result of a weak gut. The weak gut had been attributed to nutritional deficiencies and parasites. The water supply in developing countries isn't always clean and can add more challenges for someone who already has a weakened gut.

Another experience I had when I was in pharmacy school was another time I got extremely sick and I had no idea why. I hadn't been anywhere or done anything out of the norm. My lymph nodes were swollen, my jaw was tight, I couldn't eat at all, and my joints were getting stiff. I had never experienced anything like this, so it scared me. I went to visit the campus nurse and expected a full-blown course of antibiotics and/or the works. Instead, the nurse asked me just one question. She asked, "Are you stressed?" I was in shock, I hadn't planned on answering that question. After all, what did my stress have anything to do with it? I had physical symptoms that needed physical medicine, didn't I? None of this "stress talk" was going to help. I broke down in tears. The truth was, pharmacy school is very stressful. I had also lost both my grandparents in a matter of 40 days. My mom was out of town tending to the funerals and coping with her loss, so I was also in charge of running our home. I was working 3 jobs at the time and I was also going to be taking the LSATs in a month because I was considering attending law school at the time.

The nurse did give me some medicines to calm my nerves, and she also gave me some supplements and told me to go get some rest. I slept for the entire weekend, almost 20 hours, and only woke up to eat, then went straight back to bed. When I finally woke up, the swelling in my lymph nodes was gone, I felt more like myself, and learned another important lesson. The importance of rest and sleep was learned that weekend, the hard way!

I've had plenty of these experiences over the course of my journey. That's why I feel, nature is the best teacher. The symptoms we experience are nature's way of telling us that something is off. Nature is patient, it will keep putting the same situations in front of us until we learn the lesson that we are intended to learn.

I did not know the full connection between the gut and the immune system back then, but it was definitely the start of my passion. I had learned to listen to my bodily cues at a very young age. Now, I listen very intently to my clients when they tell me about their symptoms. I am a firm believer that people know when something is wrong with their bodies, and ignoring these cues is a big mistake.

After getting my doctorate in pharmacy, my next experience with holistic healing was when my husband and I were trying to start a family. We had been trying for a year but could not get pregnant. We went through all the motions of western medicine, saw fertility specialists, did all sorts of tests, and at the end of it all, everything came back as "normal." We couldn't get a diagnosis of what was wrong. We were told that since we weren't getting any younger, it would be best to move on to in vitro fertilization (IVF) since there was no other answer. At that point, a colleague at work suggested seeing a holistic healer who used ayurvedic medicine to help. Being a firm believer of western medicine at the time, I wasn't open to ayurveda but we decided to give it a shot as a last resort before moving towards IVF. We were asked to follow the ayurvedic treatment plan for 6 months, and I was pregnant in the 5th month. I had lost about 15 pounds following the ayurvedic diet and taking supplements, and my hormones were automatically balanced. That was the first time as an adult and as a pharmacist that I saw the benefits of using food and supplements as medicine. We were finally reaching our health goals, naturally.

My next encounter with functional medicine was when my son was just 6 months old and got sick for the very first time. From about 6 months to 10 months of age, we were in the ER every 2 weeks with respiratory viruses that would lead to croup and the cycle of troubled breathing. Any mom that has dealt with croup with their young ones knows just how gut-wrenching it is to see your child struggling for air. We were doing steroid treatments almost daily, and every day I would cringe at the thought of what the treatments were doing to his small lungs that were still developing. I would think about how the treatments being used to help him breathe, were actually ruining his development. I still didn't trust holistic healing at the time, at least not enough to replace those steroids that he needed to breathe. I also wasn't trained in the use of holistic health, so I didn't trust myself completely with the alternate means available for healing.

As moms, we want to do everything in our power to help our children with their struggles and it was very difficult to watch my 8-month-old child hurled over, wheezing, all because he couldn't breathe. At that moment, I would rush him outside in the cold, crisp air because I knew the cool air would help soothe him. I also started to diffuse eucalyptus oil in his humidifier to help his nasal passages to open. I would do warm cloth compresses on his tiny chest to help him to break up the cold and phlegm that built up inside his tiny body. I still didn't know much, but I knew one thing – I could no longer keep giving the inhalers and steroid treatments to my developing toddler.

We packed our bags and moved to Texas to be closer to our family, but mainly because the weather was better for his developing organs. We no longer needed to rush to the ER in the middle of the night. That's when I learned another important lesson. I learned the importance of the environment and the stress it can put on our bodies. I learned that the environment we expose ourselves to can either heal us or make us sick. The weather and the environment outside have a huge impact on what we feel inside. Now, this doesn't mean we all need to pack our bags and move somewhere warm, but it is important to recognize that if the environment outside doesn't suit our health, we need to balance it out with what we put inside our bodies. We need to be aware of our diet and use supplements to help create balance from within.

For years now, I have guided other patients, family, and friends toward natural means of healing without ever knowing that it was called functional medicine. Along the way, I have learned that western medicine's main method of treatment is to treat symptoms and not the root cause. In treating those symptoms, we are training our minds to not listen to our bodies and what it is trying to tell us. Having worked in retail, critical care in the hospital, cancer treatment centers, and everything in between, I have seen firsthand the damage caused by not treating the root cause. I am not saying we don't need western medications, however, it is a delicate balance. Once we are out of the immediate danger from acute symptoms, we need to explore the root causes of those symptoms in order to heal and not be in acute situations again. Getting to the root cause is the best option if we want to live a life of purpose and feel like we are in control of our health. It is a huge shift in mindset from how we have been doing things and where we need to be.

In 2021, I decided to get serious about studying functional medicine and realized that this was my passion all along. My goal since learning about functional medicine has been to help people with autoimmune conditions. For years, we have told people that autoimmune conditions mean a lifelong sentence where your immune system is attacking itself with no reason behind it. We have told people that there is no means to control it, besides immune-suppressing medications. I am here to spread life-giving hope to these people, as this previous way of thinking about autoimmune conditions is absolutely **NOT** true. There is always a reason why our immune system is attacking itself. There is always something that triggers our immune system to behave a certain way. Now, we can take steps to help our bodies heal. In my search to provide hope to others,

I have developed my 7-step *PATTANI*™ protocol. I aim to equip stressed, fatigued, anxious over achievers with the tools to manage their stress, have sustained energy, and live their life on their terms. When we are equipped with the correct tools, we are able to find real answers. Within my protocol, I offer specific diagnostic testing as well as 1:1 health coaching. Within just 6-12 months, each of my clients has reached their desired goals. When we work together, I teach them how to be in control of their lives and no longer label themselves as their disease.

If there is one message I wish to share with the world, it is, "You are not your disease!" From the very start, I've felt called towards helping others heal. I urge people to look into their own cultural backgrounds, and they will find that natural remedies have been around since the beginning of time. I'm sure we have all experienced times in our lives when we have chosen the natural treatment route, and also times when we've relied on western medications. Take a moment to think about what the outcomes were both times, and it is likely that you will see where real healing is found.

Today, I am aligned with my mission and vision of how I want to help the people who cross paths with me. I am ready and confident in the training I have received, and I am thrilled for what the future holds. I am excited to be embarking upon this journey where I can successfully help people get to the root cause of their symptoms and help them heal from within so that they can truly shed the label of their disease and live their best life!

ABOUT DR. DEEPA PATTANI

Dr. Deepa Pattani is a clinical pharmacy owner, Certified Functional Medicine Specialist™ from The STORRIE™ Institute, author, CBD specialist, low-dose naltrexone (LDN) compounder, wife and mom of two. Dr. Deepa equips frustrated and stressed professionals with tools to combat feelings of fatigue, anxiousness, and hopeless despair. Through her 7-Step *PATTANI Protocol™* she helps clients find sustained energy and gain back control of their control and health. In Dr. Pattani's practice, she utilizes diagnostic testing and 1:1 coaching to guide people towards whole-life wellness.

Over the past two decades, Dr. Deepa has worked in various hospitals, and long-term care facilities. Her experience has led her to the understanding that treating the root cause is the only option to achieve real healing. As an autoimmune disease educator, Dr. Deepa has helped patients manage weight loss, reduce medications, and decrease hospitalizations. She has helped over 500 patients in the last 5 years alone and is a frequent speaker and educator for other medical professionals.

Dr. Deepa has been featured in Forbes, Dallas Voyage Magazine, and twice in Authority Magazine. She has been a repeat radio guest and passionate author in the book *Creating The Functional Medicine Revolution*. She's passionate about utilizing CBD to reduce harmful effects caused by medications, as well as microdosing with low-dose naltrexone in order to reduce symptom severity in the lives of her patients.

As a leader in the holistic healing movement, Dr. Deepa is determined to never stop learning, teaching, and sharing the live-saving knowledge found through practicing functional medicine. She is on a mission to impact 1 million lives through holistic care and helping others reclaim their health.

DrDeepaPattani.com | allenpharmacist@gmail.com |
Facebook: Deepa Pattani | Instagram: @Dr.Deepa.Pattani |
Linked In: @Dr.Deepa.Pattani

Chapter 5

WELL & FREE
A MOM'S JOURNEY OF FAITH

By: Dr. Jennifer Bourgeois PharmD, IHP, CFMS

*"Your vocation in life is where your greatest joy
meets the world's greatest need."*

– FREDERICK BUECHNER

I can remember it like it was yesterday. I was 38 years old, and I was sitting on the edge of a stiff chair in front of a counselor for the first time in my life. My mind raced to make sense of what was happening and how exactly I had landed myself in this spot. She asked me a question, actually the question that would end up changing the trajectory of my life. She asked, "What makes you happy?" I couldn't respond. I was speechless. As a grown woman with multiple advanced degrees, 2 beautiful children, a loving husband, and a seemingly wonderful life, I still had no idea what made me "happy." I know my daughters love it when I paint their fingernails pink and my husband is happy when I rub his back. I know that my patients appreciate when I provide exceptional service, but as for me, I had not allowed myself to think about my own happiness because I was too preoccupied with making everyone else happy.

Sure, there was a time in my childhood when I knew what made me happy, but somewhere along the way, I lost it. I was conditioned from a young age to make decisions that made other people happy. I learned that if I was obedient, minded my manners, and got good grades in school, my parents would be pleased with me. And they would do this thing called "praise." Praise was the best! I loved the way pleasing others made me feel inside, so I practiced it daily, and I got really good at it. At some point, this behavior became a habit. My subconscious mind took over and I no longer had to think about making others happy, I just did it. My body hijacked itself, and suddenly all my decisions were based on others' emotions.

There's nothing wrong with being obedient and serving others. But my intention was to please, so all the power of that action was tied to the outcome. If I worked hard to do that "thing" and then the person didn't praise me for the action, I was crushed. Because remember, my focus was on pleasing.

Back to that stiff chair. What landed me there is complicated, but I had a moment when I realized I wasn't ok. Awareness is the first step. It was as if I'd eaten the fruit in the Garden of Eden. Everything was clear and I couldn't unsee what was being revealed. I was struggling with my mental health and I needed a professional to help me work through it. So that's exactly what I did, I found someone to help me work through it. Now, let's go back to when I sat with a counselor for the very first time and she asked me that question that changed my life.

For the first time in almost 40 years, I dreamed about what makes me happy. Hear me say this, the pursuit of happiness is not my focus. I believe chasing happiness is not beneficial to our overall well-being. When I talk about happiness in regard to my story, what I mean is recognizing what activities bring me joy and create a sense of fulfillment in my life. I also allowed myself to change this people-pleasing behavior into a God-pleasing one. I'm looking to His word to guide my actions, not to the world. I still focus on serving others, but I am no longer neglecting myself and my heart in the process. This is such an important point for all the faith-based readers out there–growing up in a religious community can create a distorted view of self. The biblical commandment actually instructs us to love others as we love ourselves. Not in a selfish way, but in a self-worth way.

Another important behavior I have changed is to focus on my intention behind why I am serving others. I shifted my intention so that I am not giving my power away. My intention is to serve and love others in a Christ-like way. Oprah said, "Intention is one with cause and effect. If your intention is to please, then you are giving your power away." On the contrary, if our intention is to serve and love, then our fulfillment isn't tied to the outcome, which is always out of our control.

I dreamed about my mission and purpose in life, and how I could align my heart's desire and divine gifts with adding value to the lives of others. Our purpose has a way of finding us, you know? It's an evolution based on our values and knowing ourselves to the fullest. Purpose doesn't have to be this big, life-changing mission. It can be for some of us. But for most of us, our purpose is to have an impact in the small areas of life. For example, a large part of my purpose is found through my testimony, my story. My story of healing my body from a chronic disease with functional medicine, and then creating a business that allows me to help others do the same. Allow me to tell you more about my personal health journey.

A few years prior, I experienced a radical change in my health. I am a high achiever who has always worked in a high-stress environment. My days were filled with constant multitasking and deadlines. I was over-scheduled, and as a result, always running late. Stress had been my reality for approximately forever. I was stuck on the hamster wheel of life and had no idea how to get off. Would the wheel ever slow down enough for me to step off? Or would I just need to jump at 60 miles per hour and hope for the best? This chronic stress wreaked havoc on my health, resulting in insomnia, headaches, and Epstein Barr virus. Epstein Barr is a viral infection that caused me to experience extreme fatigue.

For a long time, I dismissed all those symptoms as "normal." I would justify it as "I'm a working mom." My body's check engine light was on and I continued to live as though everything was fine. I also never prioritized rest. I wore the "busy badge" loud and proud! I went 90 miles per hour from sun up to sun down to get all the "working mom" things done. It was like I was waiting on someone to give me permission to take time for myself. I showed up for my family, my career, my patients, and my friends, but not for me. There was always this overwhelming guilt if I took time for myself. Rest felt as though I was just being lazy. The to-do list was a mile long, and the last thing I needed to be doing was sleeping or resting, or so I thought.

In early 2018, I remember sitting down on my couch after working a long shift in the pharmacy. The kids were playing and I could barely muster enough strength to sit upright. The fatigue was extreme. I even wondered if I would be able to get up. That was when I realized this could not be normal. I visited my primary care physician seeking answers for my ailments. "Why is this happening?" I asked him. Without asking me about my diet, exercise, or stress level, he wrote out a couple of prescriptions – one for an antidepressant and one for sleeping medicine. I was no longer ok with a prescription for a medication to treat the symptom, however, and I was looking for more. More than what he could offer me through a sick care model of medicine where insurance dictates how long we can talk and his training is to "give a pill for the ill." I left that appointment frustrated, but also empowered to use alternative solutions. I did what so many of us on this journey did – I took my health and healing into my own hands. As a result, I found integrative and functional medicine, and I loved how this practice looked specifically at the root cause. The goal was true wellness, and that's what I wanted.

After experiencing my own health transformation using functional and integrative medicine, overcoming the effects of chronic Epstein Barr infection, and rebalancing my body from chronic stress, I decided to gain additional training to become a certified practitioner myself. I completed the Integrative Health Practitioner program as well as the Functional Medicine Specialist training. Both of these certifications require specialized education and mastery of skills that allow me to work with clients in my own practice. Combining the knowledge I've gained through these certifications with my Bachelors of Science degree in nutrition and Doctorate of Pharmacy degree, empowers me with the proficiency needed to best serve my clients.

The basic concept of functional medicine is to determine how and why illness occurs and restore health by addressing the root cause. There's no quick fix or band-aid style treatment. This practice of medicine works to truly heal the person from within, which is the healthcare approach that's missing in today's broken system of sick care.

I never imagined my career would make such a pivot, but I was open to it. The personal development I had been doing for years allowed me to make changes to my mindset and habits. I began to value rest and take care of my overall well-being. Counseling offered me the opportunity to get to know myself more fully and begin to heal from the toxic behaviors of people-pleasing, codependency, and perfectionism. I also clarified my core values and embraced the idea that my mission in life is much bigger than myself. For me, success isn't defined by money or achievement, but rather by me fulfilling God's purpose for my life. As a result of these actions, I developed *Well & Free, LLC*™ to help high-achieving working moms restore their health and find true balance.

I now offer a *STRESSED MOM*™ transformation course, where we restore health and create inner peace with a science meets soul approach. Some topics covered are mindset, energy, soul care, meditation, mineral balancing, stress management, sleep hygiene, and more. It truly is a holistic approach, incorporating functional and lifestyle medicine with spirituality. Wellness encompasses emotional, mental, physical, and spiritual health, so it's important to improve resiliency in all these areas. As a high-achieving working mom myself, I know first-hand how essential all these components are to restoring health and balance.

My heart for serving in this space is to impact the lives of moms and fulfill a purpose bigger than myself. Moms need to know that life can be better than normal. I am here to inspire other moms to realize that we can show up with balance, peace, centered energy, awareness, vibrancy, and spiritual fullness. Moms are the heartbeat of the home. The glue that keeps the family together. It's time we start prioritizing our own wellness and building resilience so that we do not become unglued. Those we love the most are counting on us to take care of ourselves so we can take care of them. Without our health, we have nothing. It's time that we reclaim our lives and enjoy the blessings that we are created to experience.

ABOUT DR. JENNIFER BOURGEOIS

Dr. Jennifer Bourgeois is a Functional Medicine Specialist™ from The STORRIE™ Institute, Integrative Health Practitioner, and Clinical Pharmacist with over 15 years of experience in the health and wellness industry. After experiencing her own health transformation using functional medicine, she decided to gain additional training to become a certified practitioner herself.

Dr. Jennifer is the CEO of *Well & Free, LLC* and the founder of the *STRESSED MOM™ Transformation*. Through her practice and programs, she is able to help women restore health and discover balance with a science meets soul approach.

SingleCare recognized Dr. Jennifer as the Best Pharmacist of 2021 for her commitment to service and excellence in the profession. She has been featured in Pharmacy Times, Drug Topics, Pharmacist Moms Blog, and numerous podcasts.

In addition to her professional roles, Dr. Jennifer is the founder of a non-profit, *A New View*, that recycles and repurposes used eyeglasses. She founded her non-profit in honor of her oldest daughter, who was diagnosed with strabismus and other vision impairments at the age of one. *A New View* has given over 3,000 eyeglasses to people in need.

Dr. Jennifer is a devoted wife and mother who is passionate about wellness and her faith. She loves traveling, volunteering, and the freedom that comes along with entrepreneurship. As a high-achieving working mom herself, she knows first-hand how essential emotional, mental, physical, and spiritual wellbeing are for living a vibrant life. Dr. Jennifer is on a mission to serve busy and over-scheduled moms to help create balance through a body, mind, and soul care approach.

www.everydaypharmgirl.com | drjenbourgeois@gmail.com
Instagram: @drjenbourgeois | LinkedIn: /drjenbourgeois

Chapter 6

THE CHOICE OF FREEDOM

By: Dr. Jennifer Fernandez, PharmD, CPh, CFMP, CFMS

"Life is a matter of choices, and every choice you make, makes you."
– JOHN C. MAXWELL

When you make the decision that your life is your own to live, you choose to live it on your own terms. I spent the majority of my life feeling vibrant and full of zest. I had an undeniable desire to live with urgency and a goal to work hard to sustain a lavish lifestyle. After decades of school and practicing in my career as a pharmacist, that fast pace took its toll on my health, both physically and mentally. I noticed the obvious signs of stress at first. It looked like a few gray hairs, sore joints, and a need for a caffeine boost to get me through another workday. But over time, I started to develop other maladies that presented on my skin, through constant GI pains, mood swings, and so forth. It was my awakening.

At 34 years old, I felt like I was on a downward spiral, trying to prioritize my work ethic over my own health. I took a stand in my professional and personal life, set boundaries, and reset expectations for myself that helped me gain the life that I strived to live. It is because of my success that I am writing this now, bearing it all to the world, so that you too can find the will and the way, to break down barriers and pave your own path.

Growing up I spent a lot of time visiting different relatives who all had their own beliefs and practices around nutrition, lifestyle, career, and various definitions of success. Through my own experiences and perceptions, I observed the adults around me mimicked their actions and adopted their ways of thinking. In school, I had a strong passion for art, math, and science. I also had a lot of interest in puzzle-solving. Over time, I started to challenge the ways of my role models, always wondering why the answer to my questions was simply, "because I said so." That mentality never resonated well with me. I was a deep thinker and I liked to analyze every angle of a situation. I wanted to come to the same or an even better resolution, but by finding my own way of accomplishing the goal. As the saying goes, "There's more than one right way to do things." Up through my early 20s, life had its stressors, but nothing I couldn't handle. I could tax my body by staying up late every day, eating junk food, and working under high levels of stress without batting an eye. My body performed to my expectations, and I never gave nutrition or self-care a single thought. I had the results I wanted that whole time and never expected life to go differently.

In 2013, I hit a pivotal moment in my adult life. I had graduated from pharmacy school and started my career in helping people manage their diseases to get well. Back-to-back 13-hour shifts, harsh fluorescent lighting, the pressure to reach unrealistic performance metrics, and a small budget of tech hours were the reality of what I got with that prestigious doctorate degree. With countless doctor calls and filling hundreds of prescriptions each shift, I finally realized how many patients were not getting the help and care that I was trained to give them. I watched my favorite patients come into my pharmacy each month to pick up their prescription refills for maintenance medications. An occasional early visit or two for an acute infection was not uncommon either. And those impromptu visits gave me a chance to chat with them one on one. Aside from counseling on the key points of their current medication fill, I got to see pictures of their families, hear about their lives growing up, and learned their perspective on our current healthcare system. Those encounters, however, were few and far in between.

What I started to pick up on was their new prescriptions coming in after a scary hospital stay that came with a new deadly diagnosis if left untreated. But why was this happening? Why was I not seeing anyone get better? Sporadic and moderate symptom control was my job, apparently. I had my blinders on, and the corporate-run chain pharmacy had put them there. I wasn't allowed the time or resources to see the whole picture when it came to a patient's healthcare. The doctor made the plan, I followed the plan to the detail, and the patient also blindly complied.

Over time, this endless cycle started to get dull and I lost my passion for health and even my desire to continue within my career. I started trying to fix this by changing practice settings numerous times over the span of about 7 years, but each time the result was the same. Healthcare was a numbers-driven game, with patient outcomes and quality of life being the least important factor, if a factor at all. Days would go by, months, and then years of doing the same routine but expecting a different outcome. Hello! Can we say insanity? But that was just the start of it all.

In late 2021, I started noticing my withdrawal from society. My rigorous fitness routine had me at a plateau, my nutrition was suboptimal, and my body manifested those stressors 10-fold from all that I put it through in my 20s. I felt awful. I had my annual check-up early that year, making sure to have all the necessary blood work done to have my symptoms match a diagnosis. After all, I practice in the medical field, so there had to be a logical answer for my symptoms, right? But I was wrong. All labs came back normal. According to my doctor's office, I was perfectly healthy. Bologna! I was so fed up with feeling mentally and physically broken, and I attributed it all to my job. I kept thinking that it must just be a sign of boredom, and I let myself get complacent again.

Again, I was so very wrong! Work played a small factor, of course. But what I finally came to realize was that I was about to uncover my true calling. CBD had become very popular and I admittedly used it on a daily basis and in various forms to help with the anxiety, insomnia, soreness, and other ailments I was battling at the time. One day I started to wonder about the uses of CBD and medical marijuana. I started thinking to myself, "How could something so natural be overlooked for its wonders in treatment?" And down the rabbit hole, I went!

I spent countless hours which turned into days of research, sitting through lectures, and skimming articles when I finally stumbled upon the term, "Functional Medicine." Something so new to me has actually existed for centuries and is on the verge of becoming mainstream medicine. Many of us have been sick at some point in our lives and traditional healthcare, like that of the USA, was there to step in and "save the day!" Or so we thought. It didn't take long in my career as a pharmacist to see that we were actually doing more harm than good to our patients. Our forms of treatment are comparable to that of putting a bandaid on a gunshot wound. There is a large population of healthcare professionals who choose to practice outside the box and look for *why* sickness occurs. They spend time identifying and treating the root cause in order to prevent symptoms and disease progression. I wanted to be a part of that change and am passionate about encouraging others to explore the same path.

It was this new-found passion for healing through a whole human approach, that led me to choose to start my own functional medicine practice. I decided that in time, I would hang up my white coat and work directly with clients who feel they have exhausted all other treatment modalities and were ready to see real change. I studied, networked, hired business coaches, said a lot of prayers, and took the leap. Looking back, it has been the most liberating and gratifying thing I have done for myself.

Aside from the added freedom of no longer being a part of the corporate rat race, I have control over my schedule and client base now. Within certain legal parameters set by each individual state, I am free to work with my clients in a way that caters to their unique needs, while I avoid any unnecessary corporate red tape. At first, I set out to help people like myself. Those who felt overworked, underappreciated, and just flat-out done. But the more I learned about functional medicine, the more people I realized I could help and relate to. Athletes, stressed-out executives, stay-at-home parents, and even retirees just looking to keep active and healthy so they could spend quality time with their grandkids.

For the first time in a long time, I actually felt equipped to help someone feel truly healthy and live a better quality of life. During the launch of my business, I still worked full-time as a manager in a retail pharmacy. I committed myself to a twice-daily workout routine and still found morsels of time for a social life. I had a lot on my plate, but finding yoga and meditation was the key to my success. I learned how to be mindful and stop myself from reaching those points of burnout as I had experienced before. The techniques worked, I felt better, and I had to shout it to the world! I mapped out my journey to be a mindfulness coach and yoga instructor. If I was going to help people the way I envisioned, I was going to do it on various levels.

Your Holistic Wellness LLC™, my baby and my destiny, started off as a small idea to be a virtual health coach and educate people on living well and free. What it's turned into now is a mini-powerhouse that I plan to take on the road. Ultimately, you will find me leading wellness retreats, teaching mindfulness and yoga, and equipping my guests with the tools to experience longevity and be totally free of the box they were told to live in. What I want people to know about my way of practicing is that it is not a one-size-fits-all approach. We're done with that.

Being a middle child, I always wanted to be seen as an individual identity, not the shadow or mirror of my siblings. I had my own thoughts, perceptions, and emotions about what was going on in my surroundings. What worked for my oldest sister didn't work for me, and the same goes for my younger sister. In that same thought process, why would I want to be treated like every other patient who walked into my doctor's office for treatment? I wish to do my clients the courtesy of listening to understand and not to respond. To me, these are real people, not just a name on a medical record. There are thoughts, feelings, and emotions that I can only try to understand from their point of view, and I feel that I owe it to them to act differently than any of their medical providers ever have. These people are sick and tired of countless treatments or procedures. Has anyone done the right thing to dig deep into the individual's life-style in order to really help them? Did any of their providers actually set a goal to help them get better and not just feel better? This is the part of medicine that blows my mind. We as clinicians in the medical field are so vastly outnumbered by sick patients and limited time or resources to do any true service to our fellow human beings. Everyone I know deserves the chance at true health and wellness. The power lies within each of us to heal our bodies, but we must be shown how to use the equipment that we were all born with.

At some point in my early adult life, I made the choice to think and speak for myself. I decided to stand up against injustices and to make sure my voice was heard. When it comes to my health, I am no different. I refuse to allow a medical doctor to assign me an expiration date or turn me into another statistic. I want everyone to feel confident enough to take charge of their lives in every aspect. Career, relationships, health, everything. We are free to make choices every day, but making the best choice is often the challenge. I encourage you to dig deep, find your true self, forsake all others as no one can live your life for you. What does it look like to be free? To be happy? To be healthy? Friend, what are you waiting for? I promise you, it is never too late, and there are numerous functional medicine clinicians, just like myself, who are ready to walk you towards the healing we all deserve to have.

ABOUT DR. JENNIFER FERNANDEZ

Dr. Jennifer Fernandez is a certified Functional Medicine Practitioner through Functional Medicine University, a Certified Functional Medicine Specialist™ from The STORRIE™ Institute, and the founder of *Your Holistic Wellness LLC™*. As a practicing multi-state licensed pharmacist, she has worked in the healthcare field for 15 years and is on a mission to bring awareness to the importance of mental health and self-care. She is passionate about helping individuals who are experiencing burnout and the myriad of diseases that manifest from high stress.

Having personally experienced burnout at several points in her life, Dr. Jennifer grew "sick and tired of being sick and tired." She set out on a mission to align her passion with her profession through pursuing a career that would minimize her stress, optimize her job satisfaction, and give her a real sense of purpose. Through countless hours of researching, studying and working with business coaches, Jennifer discovered functional medicine and celebrated finding her true calling in the medical space. She realized how important it is to bring awareness and information to her clients and peers who feel 'stuck' like she once had. She believes there is power in numbers, and the more healthcare workers out there breaking into the functional medicine space, the more people we can help to stay on the path towards true health and wellness.

Your Holistic Wellness LLC™ focuses on helping individuals identify the root cause of their illnesses and work toward balance using a personalized protocol. Emphasis is placed on correcting gut health, the epicenter of imbalances throughout the body. Through mindfulness training and individualized lifestyle plans, Dr. Jennifer works with her clients by empowering them to make and maintain positive changes in their lives. She helps burned-out high performers tap into their inner peace to reclaim their mental wellbeing and overall health.

www.drjenniferfernandez.com | info@drjenniferfernandez.com |
IG: drjennimarie

Chapter 7

MY LONG AND WINDING JOURNEY

By: Dr. Joy Wright,
BSc.Phm, Pharm.D., CPh, BCPS, TTS, CFMS

*"Even the youths shall faint and be weary, And the young men
shall utterly fall, But those who wait on the Lord shall renew their strength;
They shall mount up with wings like eagles, They shall run
and not be weary, They shall walk and not faint."*

-ISAIAH 40:30-31 (NKJV)

Recently I have been thinking about what influences have occurred in my life, guidance from God, wise teachers and mentors, family and friends, and choices I have made. At the time I am writing this, the Summer Olympics are occurring and I have watched the games intently. As I see the choices they have made and the results they are achieving, I am inspired. As for myself, I have chosen to blend traditional healthcare with functional medicine, and I am intentionally taking steps forward to approach it differently than some of my colleagues. My journey is my own, but I am hoping you can learn a few things from my story that may benefit your own journey.

I have been a pharmacist for over 25 years, but ever since I was a child, I have been encouraged to explore alternative options alongside traditional healthcare. I grew up as an adopted, only child, to parents who expected the best of me. As a young child, my mom was, what I like to call, "a clean freak". I often tease her that I got bronchitis in the fall of kindergarten because my body had never been around bacteria prior to attending school. Nearly every year following, I caught respiratory illnesses, often bronchitis, resulting in needing to take a round of antibiotics. I remember being overweight at about 8 years old, and soon after, at 9 years old, I was diagnosed with scoliosis, which is the curvature of the spine from side to side. I grew up in a rural area, went to public school, and overall, lived a pretty normal life. I took piano lessons, skating lessons, sang in choirs, and performed in musicals at both school and in church. Mom took me to the chiropractor 1-2 times per week to try to straighten my back and overcome the curves. I was never very athletic, but I didn't think much about it. I got mostly A's in school and had friends and sleepovers. My life seemed pretty much like everyone else.

At age 13, I was getting ready to go camping and needed to complete a physical in June as part of the application. My family doctor had me bend over and he was shocked at how much my scoliosis had progressed. He asked my mom if I had seen the surgeon recently and what the surgeon was recommending. My parents had to admit that we never went back after the initial visit at age 9, but also told him I was working with a chiropractor, who claimed I was getting better. I was not. My family physician pushed and even though it was my parents' busy time because of their work on a fruit farm and this was all happening during harvest. They made some calls and were able to connect with a world-famous surgeon in Toronto. He worked at the Hospital for Sick Children. A referral was sent, and my appointment was scheduled for September. My chiropractor was still claiming this was a mistake and that he was helping.

At that appointment, at age 13, we found out that my scoliosis was, in fact, severe. In pictures, you could see where my clothes didn't fit right, as my shoulders and hips were off-center. The physician took x-rays and then told my parents and I that if I had come at age 9, we could have discussed bracing or even later less invasive muscle stimulators. At this point, however, my only option was to be fully fused. I had both an upper and lower curve, so my spine looked like an "S". The physician looked at me that day and I will never forget what he said. He told me, "Without surgery, you will be the humpback of Notre Dame by 20, bedridden due to your organs being crushed by 30, and dead by 40 years old." Even though I was only 13, he told me it was not my parents' decision, but that I had to make the choice of how to proceed since it was my life. I chose surgery.

Originally, the surgery was planned for February, but we got a call at the beginning of November that a cancellation had opened a spot for me. My surgery was quickly set for November 15th. I was admitted to the hospital 2 days before the surgery for testing, where we found out from comparing the results from tests in September, that my curves were advancing at 3 degrees per month. If my surgery had been in February, they would not have been able to fully straighten me. Talk about God's perfect timing. My curves were at 57 degrees (upper) and 60 degrees (lower) and that is the maximum amount that is able to be straightened. The surgery took several hours, as they had to put in 2 rods and 8 clamps that had been specially designed by the surgeon and his engineer son. They used specialized equipment, based on the Herrington Rod fusion procedure. My surgeon went around the world teaching this method to other surgeons. In the testing, we found out my spine had already started to crush my lungs, as my breathing capacity was less than expected. This could have impacted why I so frequently got bronchitis both before and after the surgery. In the surgery, I gained 3 inches in height. This all happened during my 8th-grade year. I was homeschooled with tutors from the county for about 2-3 months, and then went back to school and finished out the school year. I was not allowed to do anything physical, including bending over for the first 3 months, and then after that, slowly went back to normal activities once I reached the one-year point. No one, at that time, ever mentioned physical therapy. However, throughout the surgery and recovery, my mom proclaimed the verses from Isaiah (also at the beginning of my chapter), over me. She declared that I would achieve health and mobility again through faith and perseverance, which I did.

In high school, I still excelled in academics. I stacked my schedule in order to finish Grade 13 by the end of Grade 12. I graduated with 7 credits (6 was the usual) and other than the mandatory English class, my other 6 classes were 3 math (Relations and Functions, Algebra, and Calculus) and 3 science classes (Chemistry, Biology, and Physics). During Grade 10, I had met with the guidance counselor and was told, due to my abilities in math and chemistry, I should consider chemical engineering or pharmacy as a profession. In Grade 11, I was able to get a job as a cashier for a chain pharmacy about 20 minutes from home. I learned about OTC (over-the-counter) medications by stocking shelves and focusing on customer service as a cashier. The more I learned about pharmacy, the more I realized it was a good career choice for me. By the end of Grade 12, however, after being treated unfairly by the associate-owner, I knew that a chain pharmacy was not where I wanted to end up. I am grateful for the opportunities I had and for parents who expected great things from me, and the minimum standard would be a university degree and a profession to call my own.

Not only was my family a big proponent of alternative therapies like chiropractic adjustments and herbal supplements, but also, my paternal grandfather almost died of a heart attack while I was in middle school and ended up using chelation therapy. I never realized at the time how controversial things like that were to other people because to me, they were just accepted as other beneficial alternatives. Chelation therapy is receiving intravenous medications to bind heavy metals like lead, mercury, and iron and was considered an off-label treatment for cardiovascular disease. This means it was not scientifically validated to provide benefit for heart disease and could actually be harmful since it was not tested for this use. While he seemed to derive some benefit from it, it is no longer recommended since some people can have side effects from this, and some of them can be severe and include death. Alongside this, he also drastically changed his lifestyle by limiting sodium and walking daily.

As I mentioned earlier, it was never a question of whether I was going to go to university. I knew from the beginning that I was going to go. I just got to choose which program I attended. At the end of Grade 12, I received acceptance letters for both chemical engineering and pharmacy programs. It was then that I realized that my heart was in pharmacy. At the graduation ceremony, my school surprised me by awarding me the Chemistry Scholarship that was funded by a local pharmacy. They announced that in the many years it had been given, I was the first to get it and actually be accepted to pharmacy school.

Pharmacy school also encouraged me to incorporate alternative models of healing, along with usual healthcare. In our fourth, and final year, we chose electives and an honors project. As my electives, I chose self-medication (which covered OTC products, vitamins, and herbal supplements), drug information (how to critically evaluate literature and write abstracts), and First Nations Healing practices. This is where I was taught, for 10 weeks, by a native healer and it also included a trip to her farm to see how she grew, dried, and used herbs and plants in her practice. My honors project advisor was a Ph.D. social scientist, so we also worked on a questionnaire for practicing pharmacists and pharmacy students. This questionnaire focused on identifying their beliefs and implementation, personally, of alternative healing models. This included herbal supplements, prayer and meditation, chelation therapy, and other modalities popular at that time.

Throughout my career as a pharmacist, I have had lots of different experiences and health issues that have shaped my opinions and recommendations, including both the use of traditional medications, lifestyle changes, and nutritional supplements. During the 10 years I worked in Canada, I worked in a variety of independent community pharmacies and had the opportunity to become a compounding pharmacist (certified through Professional Compounding Centers of America). I also taught at the college level to pharmacy technician students, teaching them about traditional drugs and herbal products. I also had opportunities in leadership, getting involved in local, provincial, and national pharmacy associations.

Another one of the activities I did in Canada that not only shaped me but that I am proud of accomplishing, was getting involved as a speaker for the Osteoporosis Foundation of Canada. If any public group, church group, or other entity reached out and wanted a lecture on Osteoporosis, we were trained to give 1-2 hour talks on the prevention and treatment of Osteoporosis. Again, a very prominent part of Osteopenia and Osteoporosis prevention and treatment is a lifestyle. Incorporating high calcium foods like dairy, vitamin D supplementation, limiting alcohol and smoking, and choosing exercise for strengthening and building bones were important aspects of prevention. I have spoken to small groups and audiences of up to 350 people, not only in Canada, but also in the US.

As I said before, lifestyle can be a huge factor in the prevention and treatment of Osteoporosis. The goal for dietary calcium should be 1000 mg elemental calcium per day, and vitamin D should be at least 800 international units (20mcg) per day, however, I prefer checking vitamin D levels and increasing daily supplementation to get to at least 50 ng/dl which is in the middle of the accepted normal range. Vitamin D is made in our skin by exposure to the sun but with sunscreen use, our skin is prevented from making it and even if someone doesn't wear sunscreen, most people do not get enough skin exposure or time outside per week to make enough. Most people are vitamin D insufficient or deficient (under 30ng/dl). Fatty fish can also be a good source of vitamin D, but most of us do not eat this on a daily basis. Other lifestyle changes like limiting alcohol, caffeine, quitting smoking, and making sure you do not have any fall hazards in the home can also help reduce risk. Weight-bearing exercise is the only lifestyle activity that will actually build bone. This includes using your own body weight or adding weight to exercises like weight lifting, jumping, running, or high-intensity interval walking where you change pace and incline on a regular basis. Yoga, Tai Chi, and other stretching-type exercises are great for improving balance in order to prevent falls and are also highly recommended.

Soon after graduation from pharmacy school, with my Bachelor's of Science degree in Pharmacy, my husband and I started talking about moving from Canada to the southern US. I am not a fan of cold and snow, which I often blame on the metal in my back, and my husband didn't like shoveling snow. As I looked into practicing pharmacy in the US, I realized I would need a Doctor of Pharmacy degree to be competitive for the jobs that most interested me. I ended up completing my Doctor of Pharmacy degree using a university with a Non-Traditional program that could be done mostly in Canada, but was still able to graduate with a

US degree in 2001 from Shenandoah University in Winchester, Virginia. I took the licensing exams in 2002 and ended up moving to the US in 2004.

My first position in the United States required a consultant pharmacy license, which I obtained as soon as I was able to, in the first year. I then was hired by a hospital system to work inside the hospital, which taught me so much about injectable medications that I'd only heard of in lectures before that. I realized I loved patient care, and soon became Board Certified, and moved into a clinical pharmacist position after just a couple of years. Throughout my years of helping transplant patients, patients with autoimmune issues, and trying to keep patients out of the hospital, I have gained a lot of experience. I have become very familiar with using traditional medications, lifestyle changes, and supplements needed to help patients get to the goals they set out to achieve. I have not, however, always taken care of myself in the same manner, which is why I am now on this journey towards becoming certified in functional medicine. I realize this will help me to take my knowledge to the next level, start implementing these changes into my own life, and help others as I try to assist in their implementation. I am a good listener, and I hope my patients hear my empathy through my voice, knowing how hard it is to not only make dietary and lifestyle changes, but to know that I too, am working to eat out less, limit sodium, focus on vegetables and proteins, and try to limit sugar, which is my nemesis.

Functional medicine just makes sense to me. I don't want to abandon well-proven medications for lowering blood pressure, reducing cardiovascular risks, treating diabetes, etc. But I also feel all conditions will be improved by eating healthier, adding safe exercises, reducing alcohol, tobacco, and sugar. I am excited to learn about labs that can identify food sensitivities that I may not be aware of, and assist others with the same issues I struggle with. I love educating people about their diseases, conditions, and medications, and already incorporate vitamin counseling if the patient is interested. I am very grateful to have worked with a pharmacist in Canada, who was a world-renown speaker and author on vitamin deficiencies and natural therapies. Her practice impacted mine and now I often recommend B complex vitamins and magnesium to help with managing stress, low doses of zinc for immunity and mental capacity, as well as other nutritional supplement recommendations that I learned and incorporated from my time working with her. As a compounding pharmacist, I was exposed to bioidentical hormone replacement and the benefits of these products, over some of the synthetic options that many of the studies were based on. Again, these products are not for everyone, and in fact, I feel this is one of the areas that Western Medicine can falter. By using drugs broadly, instead of determining the right (personalized) combination for each person, we are not helping to solve the problem for the patient. I am excited about the advances being made in pharmacogenomics to take personalized medicine to the next level so before you take a medication, you can know what side effects you are more likely to have than someone else, or even if you will respond to that therapy. This helps us to know if other options would be better for the individual.

I just recently started my business, and am slowly incorporating a wellness philosophy in all that I do. I provide a way for my clients to have access to some low sodium, clean eating spice blends, to make their food taste good, and also focus on recipes using high-quality ingredients in a quick and healthy way. I am also working on building a team of health care professionals that can provide labs and counseling that support Functional Medicine. I am excited to share everything that I learn as I complete my Functional Medicine certification program. Not only am I thrilled to be working with people with autoimmune issues and hyperinsulinemia, but I will also continue to expand my message on the prevention of osteoporosis, in addition to incorporating lifestyle changes, both small and big, to all that I work with. I look forward to adding team members that can address addiction, mental health, and other health issues that I am passionate about, bringing healing to patients and clients who are currently struggling in these areas.

Some may question why I want to set up a team of professionals for this business. Most are used to one-on-one coaching type models or in-class type instruction. I have seen the benefit of having many health professionals come together, bringing their unique perspectives to solve the many issues in healthcare. By having a physician who is the diagnostic expert, the pharmacist who is the drug and supplement expert, the social worker who can delve into the social determinants of health and provide resources when needed, the mental health counselor to address issues like anxiety, insomnia, motivation, and many others, the patient will get the optimal healthcare and plan. The patient will finally be able to implement and accomplish the goals that they set and want to achieve. By working as a team, when roadblocks are encountered, the many perspectives can work on problem-solving with the patient's input to come up with a new plan. By looking at life as a journey to wellness, the team can come alongside to assist and guide, while the patient can direct what goals are the priority at this moment. Too often I have seen the prescriber want to use only traditional medications when the patient wanted a more holistic approach. Or the opposite, the prescriber wanted to rely on lifestyle changes, when the patient was not ready at that moment, to implement the plan the physician gave them. By focusing on the priorities of the patient, the plan can be adjusted and molded to fit each person's unique desires, and truly become the personalized medicine model that they need.

Many talk about improving healthcare, however, I think until the patient is at the center of a team model, it will be very hard to accomplish any change in the US healthcare system. Without incorporating all the tools we have, including lifestyle changes, medications, gathering multiple perspectives, expanded labs, and using supplements, we will not be able to help patients achieve their desired outcomes. It is extremely important to be looking at how we can live lives that are less taxing on the environment, use less toxic products in our everyday life for personal hygiene and cleaning, eat more organic proteins, healthy vegetables, and incorporate movement appropriately for our physical health. Practicing functional medicine is the gateway to achieving the healthcare system so many of us desperately need and want. This is the very reason I have chosen to walk down this long and winding journey towards helping others and myself, achieve our wellness goals necessary in order to live healthy and joy-filled lives.

ABOUT DR. JOY WRIGHT

Dr. Joy Wright is a licensed pharmacist, having held positions in community pharmacy, hospital pharmacy, and academia in both Canada and the United States over the last 30 years. She is also licensed as a consultant pharmacist in the state of Florida. Dr. Joy is board certified in Pharmacotherapy Specialties and has certificates in compounding, Medication Therapy Management, and as a Tobacco Treatment Specialist. As she has discovered the healing power of functional medicine, she has become a Certified Functional Medicine Specialist™ from The STORRIE™ Institute and is working on an additional certification through the Functional Medicine University.

In her current practice, Dr. Joy assists patients with lifestyle changes and comprehensive medication reviews to ensure every medication is necessary, effective, safe, and appropriate for the patient. She also recommends vitamins and supplements to help patients meet their health goals. She enjoys working with physicians, social workers, dentists, mental health professionals, occupational therapy, nurses, and other health care professions so the patient can get the unique benefit of many perspectives and use the principles of functional medicine to get to the root cause of disease.

Dr. Joy is aware of the impact social determinants of health can have on patient care and the barriers it can create for patients in their health care journey. A team approach, through having social workers and mental health practitioners on the team, can make overcoming the barriers and providing resources to the patient much more accessible. Now, Dr. Joy has started her own functional medicine practice and is working one-on-one with clients to help them achieve their health goals. Her dream is to have an in-person wellness center for patients to have access to all the professionals they may need to reclaim their health.

Dr. Joy has spoken to small and large groups, both in the community and professionally, about weight loss and obesity, diabetes, osteoporosis, socialized medicine, the dangers of drug importation and counterfeit drugs, and much more. She is an active member of her local, state, and national pharmacy associations, holding a variety of leadership positions over the years. She mentors many students who have chosen the path to become pharmacists to help guide them in their career direction, whether it be through working, residency, or fellowship. She has contributed to books, medical journals, and newsletters, primarily in the medical profession.

www.epicjoyhealth.com | drjoyannawright@gmail.com | LinkedIn: Joy Wright

Chapter 8

FROM PAIN TO PURPOSE

By: Dr. Judy Magalhaes, PharmD, BCGP, CDCES, CFMS

"There is no medicine like HOPE, no incentive so great, and no tonic so powerful as expectation of something better tomorrow."
– ORISON SWETT MARDEN

Do you believe everything happens for a reason? If so, do you believe you are exactly where you are supposed to be? It took me 30 years to figure it out for myself, but eventually, it happened. I am exactly where I am supposed to be. My purpose has finally been revealed – to help others who are tired of being sick and who are failing to heal their bodies through using pharmaceuticals, to embrace a happier and healthier life.

During the last few years, we have all been experiencing a global pandemic. At the start of this time, I was working as a consultant pharmacist in long-term and primary care settings. It quickly became grueling work. Like so many healthcare providers, I too felt a sense of helplessness, as we worked without established guidelines or protocols to treat a virus we had never encountered before. Apprehension and exhaustion overtook us all. Helping patients navigate through a system that had shifted from face-to-face interactions and physical exams to phone calls or telehealth visits was excruciating for all entities involved. The patients lacked the ability and resources to even participate much of the time. Providing care and support to the patients we couldn't see or touch felt cold and even cruel. And yet, we knew we had no choice but to try and adapt. The pressure was mounting.

By August 2020, I was back working in the office and started seeing patients who continued to struggle with chronic diseases and were returning for evaluation and medication management. Sadly, many were worse after months of isolation and lockdowns. They were unable or unwilling to see their doctors, leave their house, or manage basic needs like nutrition and self-care. Their symptoms worsened with the burden of being alone, their diseases, raging anxiety, and overall poor health status. At times, it felt hopeless. I continued working in long-term and primary care throughout the fall and early winter of 2020. December 23rd was my last day of work before Christmas. While I was eager for the holidays, due to COVID-19 concerns, we would not see most of our relatives, deciding instead to limit our gathering to just immediate family. This Christmas was different, and I realized how truly exhausted I had become. When everyone returned to work on Monday, December 28th, I realized I was no longer able to join them.

It started with a headache. My back hurt, and that weariness had overtaken me. Was it merely post-holiday fatigue? Perhaps hormone disruption? At that point, my menstrual cycle was erratic and unpredictable, with two months passing since the last. My doctor ordered blood work that indicated I was post-menopausal. Still, my health status continued to deteriorate.

By the next day, Tuesday, I was so much worse. My headache morphed into a migraine with severe light and noise sensitivity that I had never before experienced. I was sapped of energy, unable even to get out of bed. My back pain intensified to the point where I couldn't bear to be touched. My entire body was aflame with agony, and I was desperate for relief. Then, during this incredible physical plummet, my period arrived with debilitating ferociousness. But, how could this be? I was supposed to be post-menopausal, right?

A family member called to check in on me. She was watching *The Ellen DeGeneres Show,* as the host described similar symptoms of excruciating back pain and extreme fatigue while she battled COVID-19. I wondered, could it be? Could I, too, have contracted this virus? Why now? After almost one full year on the front lines of healthcare, why had it taken this long? And my biggest question of all, how did the virus break through all of my protective practices? I called my doctor and asked for a test. On Wednesday, New Year's Eve of 2020, I received my results. I was positive for COVID-19!

I began my ten-day quarantine on New Year's Day 2021. I had notified the doctor and staff as well as the patient I saw on my last day of work of my diagnosis. Within a few days, I was informed the patient was hospitalized with COVID-19, and a few days later, the doctor was admitted to the hospital as well. The news shattered me, as a deep concern grew for the well-being of them both. Even as I exited quarantine, symptoms remained. While tolerable, they were troubling and constant, leaving me unable to return to work or connect with the ailing doctor. I anxiously waited for news, but when it came, it was mortifying. After six weeks of hospitalization, both the patient and doctor had declined, with one requiring transfer to the ICU for intubation due to respiratory distress, and the other developing complications. Within one week, both had died.

This broke me. As sobs wracked my body, I had undeniable questions – why and how.

My grief spiraled to a new low, I was overcome with sadness and hopelessness, and the worst of the symptoms I was trying to recover from, had returned. What was happening to me?

Was this normal grieving? Survivor's guilt? The effects of lingering COVID-19 symptoms? My head pounded and I could not think or function. Brain fog crept in, and a fuzzy, dull space of emptiness and angst lingered within me. Fatigue gripped my body. I had no energy, and the concept of returning to work seemed unimaginable.

According to the CDC[1], "some people experience a range of new or ongoing symptoms that can last for weeks or months after first being infected with the virus." Unlike some other types of post-COVID conditions that occur in people who have underlying comorbidities or have experienced severe illness, post-COVID symptoms can happen to anyone who has had COVID-19. No matter the severity, even if the illness was mild or if they had no initial symptoms, every person is subject to the long-term effects including fatigue, shortness of breath, difficulty concentrating, sleep disorders, fevers, anxiety, and depression. Aside from the shortness of breath, sleeping problems, and fevers, I was experiencing all of these symptoms.

Doctors offered prescriptions to help manage my symptoms. Anti-depressants, pain medications, anti-anxiety agents, and even steroid injections for back pain. I rejected it all, knowing I did not want to put a band-aid on my symptoms or become dependent. I sought another way, a more holistic and natural approach to symptom relief that would also help me to reclaim my health and restore my mind to its productive state. I reached out to a colleague I met at the beginning of the pandemic, Daryl Hill. Daryl immediately sensed how unwell I had become. He could feel the grief, tiredness, anxiety, and dulled brain, even as I held back the depth of emotions that had enveloped my life. But then, it happened.

The well of tears emptied and I poured out my story of loss, fear, pain, and bewilderment. He was empathetic and sincere, even sharing some of his own experiences with survivor's guilt and PTSD. He told me how he worked with veterans, active service members, and people who suffer from anxiety or post-traumatic stress. He explained how he assists them in healing through meditation and mindset (aka The D.A.R.T. Method)[2]. When he offered a private session, I accepted immediately. I had nothing to lose, and despite never having tried meditation or mindfulness techniques before, I promised myself I would give this an honest effort. And while none of these aspects of wellness were part of my education or clinical training in pharmacy, I was intrigued and duty-bound to try, because, at that time, my life depended on the ability to have faith in something brand new.

How grateful I am now that I listened to that voice inside. Turns out, it was right! The very next night, we spent two hours together on the phone with me lying down on my bed, lights off, door locked, and my phone on the nightstand beside me. My friend Daryl guided me through a form of deep meditation. It reminded me of *conscious sedation*, a procedure with intravenous (IV) medications to induce sleep, typically used in the ICU for patients on ventilators. He spoke softly, directing my breathing in a pattern of holding and releasing that gave my brain permission to journey back to places I loved and memories I cherished the most. The beach, vacations, holidays, time with my family, all good memories. I was then directed to release the sadness, guilt, and pain in order to illuminate the happy and good. My finest moments and future dreams miraculously appeared. I could visualize new goals. Tears ran down my face. A chill swept through my body, and my chest felt heavy. When I came back to the present and opened my eyes, I was back in the present but felt different. I felt relaxed and at peace. The present was actually quite nice. A feeling that I had been desperately longing for, for some time.

We spoke briefly afterward and he informed me that I will continue to heal and my subconscious mind will take over in the days and weeks ahead. Daryl said, "It may take some time, but you will begin to feel better each day." I was skeptical, but hopeful because I so badly wanted my life back. I remember waking up the next morning on a Saturday in February, during full winter in New England, and yet, for some reason, I had an urge to go for a walk. I coaxed my husband and dog Leo into joining me. Wearing my warmest jacket, hat, gloves, and sneakers, we headed out into the freezing cold. Within ten minutes, it started to snow. Beautiful large snowflakes landed upon my face and planted on top of my eyelashes. I stuck out my tongue to catch some as my husband snapped a picture. In it, I was smiling, almost as though my body was revealing an alteration from within. I knew then that something powerful had happened the night before. My friend had thrown a rope down to me in that dark and deep hole that I was in. He'd taught me how to climb out. He showed me how to get better, just like he said I would.

Fixing myself first became my priority at this point. I knew that if I could function better, I could truly help others. I had to give myself permission to focus on my own self-care, and not succumb to the pressure, stress, and demands of working in healthcare. Like so many, I sacrificed my health and well-being by enduring long hours of intense, life or death roles, forgoing sleep, and sacrificing my own health. I had deprived myself and my family for too long, and it was time for me to say, "no more!"

My health became my priority, and while brain fog and headaches were improving, my fatigue and back pain persisted. There were days the pain hit so dramatically, I could not walk. Even lying flat at night, the twinges down my spinal cord and along my nerves felt like an enveloping fire. I had experienced back pain and sciatica in the past from trauma and motor vehicle accidents that exacerbated my underlying spinal condition (spondylolisthesis). This was different though, this pain was more intense and persistent. Ice and chiropractic manipulation provided some relief, but only temporarily, and each time the pain would return. Finally, when I could no longer bear it, I went to see my doctor. With tears in my eyes and obvious discomfort, he immediately understood the severity. He offered me pain medications, muscle relaxants, and antidepressants. He ordered some labs and imaging tests. Unaware of my history of spondylolisthesis, he referred me to an orthopedic specialist. After reviewing my labs and images, the orthopedist explained my options: I could have steroid injections and hope for temporary relief (for weeks or months) or spinal surgery to repair the defect in my lumbar spine. Both had risks that I was not willing to accept, and surgery was definitely a last resort I prayed I would never need. After all this, I still did not have any answers as to *why* my back, was so inflamed, or simply *why* I was in so much pain. Nothing made sense, I had no recent trauma or injury to explain it but I knew there was something wrong. I decided to try physical therapy in search of a way to better support my spine without drugs and surgery. At least this seemed to be a "risk-free" option, and just like with seeing Daryl, I suspected it may work. Guess what? My instincts were right, it did work.

In physical therapy, I began learning exercises to strengthen my core, improve lifting and bending techniques, and support my lumbar spine, which was just what I needed. In two months, I had made great progress and significantly reduced the severity and frequency of my pain. My next step was to find a health coach. I was ready to experience a full lifestyle transformation and reclaim my health from within.

I already knew that years of stress and hormonal changes had contributed to my emotional and physical symptoms. I had also gained weight, despite restricting calories and putting in many hours on the elliptical. My BMI had crept into the overweight category. Both my doctor and I knew of the risks contained in that: hypertension, high cholesterol, and diabetes. Had I become the patient we treated every day in the office? I could not fathom these unacceptable circumstances.

I received my orders for diet modifications and increased my exercise and physical activity, but wasn't I already doing these? I couldn't help but wonder if there were other reasons for my weight gain. There had to be. While I was otherwise healthy, my body was under stress and my hormones were out of balance. Post COVID-19 conditions were a factor, too. So much to consider as I sought new and evolving solutions.

By August 2021, I was making great progress in my transformation and had decided to invest more into a personal health coach and program. I was feeling better and understanding more about my body's unique needs. I approached nutrition by examining a proper understanding of balance. Carbohydrates, protein, and fats are needed to support cardio and strength-building exercises. I put in the time and educated myself on what I put into my body. Sure enough, I began to lose weight and feel better! I was on the right track and continued to improve my health and wellbeing. Now, it was time to look for a job.

My resume got a makeover, and I applied for positions like clinical pharmacist, diabetes educator, and lifestyle coach. During my job search, I discovered a post by Dr. Christine Manukyan, PharmD, MS. She was offering a program to help pharmacists and other healthcare professionals leave their high-stress corporate jobs to become functional medicine practitioners and entrepreneurs. She was inviting clinicians to join her

Functional Medicine Business Academy. It felt like a calling and I enrolled immediately.

Functional Medicine is a fascinating practice, and I instantly saw how it differs from conventional medicine and what we know as *healthcare* today. Functional medicine is a systems biology-based approach that focuses on identifying and addressing the root cause of disease[3]. During my three decades of pharmacy practice, I had developed a deep understanding of pathophysiology (disordered physiological processes) and how medications work to treat or manage conditions. I had this knowledge but I never went deeper than the drug mechanisms of action in order to connect this with the root cause of symptoms. If only I had asked why a patient was experiencing symptoms such as headaches, rashes, congestion, or allergy flare-ups, instead of merely diagnosing them with allergies and prescribing antihistamines, steroids, and bronchodilators, I may have arrived at a different place. The *why* was lost, and it struck me as an utter waste of what could be immensely valuable information in attaining wellness. In traditional medicine, we are trained to diagnose and treat with medications, rather than seek the root cause. The *why* is often ignored completely.

This stirred up even more questions. Was it really that simple, though? Could the *why* of my unhealthiness really be caused by a complete disregard for the root cause of mine and so many other's symptoms? Was something inside our bodies not working and they were sending out signals in a desperate attempt to tell us? These questions led to the moment I had been waiting for, my epiphany!

To test out my theory, I began running functional medicine tests on myself, seeking detailed information and knowledge about what was really going on within my body. I had to know the root causes of my symptoms before I could truly understand the healing power of functional medicine. Why had I suffered so much in the past year? Had everything been caused by COVID-19 or were there other underlying reasons?

The notion of fixing myself to become a better practitioner became paramount. I tested my mineral status and toxic element exposure first. I learned I had an excess of copper in my tissues and that affected other essential elements (vitamins and minerals) that were responsible for energy production, iron metabolism, neuropeptide activation, connective tissue synthesis, and neurotransmitter synthesis[4]. Was this the root cause of all my ailments: allergies, anemia, hormone imbalance, thyroid, arthritis, dermatitis, fatigue, depression, and headaches? I also wondered if this played a role in my spondylolisthesis and the severe pain I had for months after COVID-19. Was copper toxicity the root cause? I am now convinced it played a significant role because shortly after starting a regimen of supplements and detoxification, most of my symptoms resolved or were reduced considerably. I no longer needed my antihistamine or nasal steroid for my allergies. I haven't had any back pain requiring medication or trips to the chiropractor. My energy improved and I was able to lose weight upon learning how my metabolism had become altered by the imbalances in my tissues (not in my blood). Had I not tested and confirmed this, it could have progressed to the liver or other neurological diseases.

If you're like me, you would want to know how and why this copper toxicity occurred. After ruling out the copper pipes within my water supply as a source, I did some research on food. I was shocked to find out that my so-called healthy diet was high in copper. Did you know the richest dietary copper sources include shellfish, seeds and nuts, organ meats, mushrooms, avocado, tofu, chickpeas, whole-grain products, and chocolate[5]? I sure didn't! And those who know me best would confirm I am a lobster-loving chocoholic who indulged in hearty portions of nuts, seeds, and avocado as well. These were all the alleged "healthy foods"

I consumed regularly and even increased in my diet since I had begun working with a health coach.

I think the most important lesson I learned in my journey is that one size will never fit all. It has been an unforgettable and humbling experience to personally feel the power of our uniqueness and how everything affects each of us differently, both inside and out. I could finally unravel the widely held concept that "cook-book medicine" is built for the good of the entirety. No! That's not true! Instead, it should be sectioned off and used as individualized best practice. We need to test and not guess! Respecting our uniqueness should be the first step, rather than accepting the latest fad sweeping across TV or social media as the "fix-all" to our sicknesses. What your family member or best friend is taking for some symptoms or presumed benefit may actually be harmful to you. Your biochemistry must be understood and protected, and Functional Medicine thrives to meet you in that goal.

My professional development was not a straight and narrow course, more like taking the scenic route with lots of detours, lay-overs, and adventures. My experience, pain, and suffering brought me to Functional Medicine and finding the root cause of many of my symptoms. Maybe getting COVID-19 was the start of this transformation. Maybe it was the wake-up call I didn't know I needed that was telling me to slow down, take care of myself, and find my purpose. I finally understood that the trials and tribulations were necessary in order for me to become who I am today.

Ultimately, my epiphany gave rise to my purpose. That clarity supplied insight into why, after thirty years of practicing clinical pharmacy in the conventional medicine system, I recommitted myself to educating and empowering people to reclaim their health through natural and holistic options, without pharmaceuticals. My method starts with an individualized approach to help people suffering from stress, fatigue, and chronic disease through targeted testing with an emphasis on the importance of "test don't guess." I provide hope to all those who want to find the root cause of their symptoms or conditions and reclaim their health through holistic options (not pharmaceuticals) so they too can live happier and healthier lives.

My suffering spawned a new strength. The mental, physical, and emotional anguish pushed me into a new realm at the time that I was most open and willing to accept it. To rebuild, but better this time, and in a more complete way to impact the world around me. Without the fall, I could never have found the desperation to reveal the *why*. And, the *why* has changed my life. I have found the root causes, and I am finally healing. I am grateful for my evolution, and for what I have learned at every turn. Special thanks to my husband and family for tolerating me when I was at my lowest point. When my health had tanked and I was but a flicker of dulled light. You all gave me hope, and you helped me so I could find my way back to life again.

Learn from yesterday, live for today, hope for tomorrow.
The important thing is not to stop Questioning.
– ALBERT EINSTEIN

References:

1. *COVID-19 and Your Health*. (2020, February 11). Centers for Disease Control and Prevention. https://www.cdc.gov/coronavirus/2019-ncov/long-term-effects/index.html

2. Hill, D. (2020, March 5). *Services »*. Daryl HIll. https://darylhill.com/

3. *What is Functional Medicine? | IFM.* (2021, October 28). The Institute for Functional Medicine. https://www.ifm.org/functional-medicine/what-is-functional-medicine/

4. Jewell, T. (2019, March 8). *What to Know About Copper Toxicity.* Healthline. https://www.healthline.com/health/copper-toxicity#-foods-list

5. *Office of Dietary Supplements - Copper.* (2021, March 29). National Institute of Health. https://ods.od.nih.gov/factsheets/Copper-HealthProfessional/#h8

ABOUT DR. JUDY MAGALHAES

D r. Judy Magalhaes is a Certified Functional Medicine Specialist™ from The STORRIE™ Institute, Board-Certified Geriatric Pharmacist, Lifestyle Coach, and Diabetes Care & Education Specialist. She is the CEO & Founder of Holistic Options & Personal Empowerment™, LLC (HOPE) offering a multi-faceted program to provide relief from burnout, stress, fatigue, and chronic disease. HOPE uses a transformative approach to target the restoration of health and wellbeing in both body and mind.

For more than 30 years, Judy has worked in multiple healthcare settings ranging from hospitals, community, long-term and primary care in order to collaborate with providers and patients to optimize medication regimens, reduce adverse reactions, and manage chronic diseases. In addition to her many achievements in quality and safety initiatives, provider-patient satisfaction, and improving medication adherence, Judy was also recognized as "Preceptor of the Year" by Massachusetts College of Pharmacy and Health Sciences (MCPHS) pharmacy interns, for her mentorship in the acute care setting.

Even as she thrived in this award-winning career, Judy felt the toll of her high-stress and demanding job as a clinical pharmacy manager and began to see it as the probable "root cause" of her own declining health and chronic symptoms. She sought new ways to improve her health without prescription medications or surgical interventions. It was during this time of research and reflection that Judy discovered functional medicine and subsequently used it to transform her own health through lifestyle changes and nutrition.

As she closely examined her decades spent working in the healthcare system, Judy developed an awareness and realization that even with modern medical interventions and medications, people stayed sick, and their battles with chronic diseases waged on and were often attributed to age or bad genes. More medications were doled out to control symptoms and a "prescribing cascade" ensued, elevating risks of adverse effects, drug interactions, toxicities, and nutrient deficiencies. Judy watched people take excess medications and yet they remained ill. She knew there was a better way.

As a Functional Medicine practitioner, Dr. Judy understands there is no magic pill to treat symptoms or diseases. What works for some, may cause harm to others. She is passionate about helping people identify the root causes of their symptoms, unravel their origins, and then use them to optimize their health and quality of life. Her focus is on individualized, targeted therapies based on each person's unique needs, rather than the overused one-size-fits-all standardized approach of care many are becoming unsatisfied with.

Dr. Judy is thrilled to bring her experience and passion to this new realm. Through expertise and her own personal journey, she is excited to deploy her knowledge and wisdom to help patients restore good health through holistic options and functional medicine practices.

www.drjudym.com | Instagram: @drjudymagalhaes
Facebook Group: www.facebook.com/groups/hopewithdrjudy
LinkedIn: dr-judy-magalhaes-hope-llc-founder-75952849

Chapter 9

GENERATIONAL BLESSING OF ENTREPRENEURSHIP

By: Dr. Kellye Schab, PharmD, CFMS

"Your value will not be what you know; it will be what you share."
– GINNI ROMETTY, CEO, IBM

I was in the height of my reproductive years when I started working with women at the end of theirs. It was intimidating and let's just say, I was terrified! How was I supposed to educate these women who have had life experiences that I had yet to learn? What could I possibly teach them about their bodies that they didn't already know? These were the questions that ricocheted in my mind.

It was the summer of 2006, and I had just stepped into a new job at a pharmacy after moving with my infant daughter and husband. This locally owned "mom and pop" pharmacy had quite a large presence in the community, and they offered a variety of services and products in order to best serve the small-town population. They hired me to be their Compounding Pharmacist and I worked primarily with patients needing hormone, nutritional, and preventative guidance. My education and prior work experience never exposed me to this side of medicine, so I had a lot to learn. I found out later that many medical professionals never get the opportunity to learn about preventive care or hormone health. I had no idea at the time that this opportunity would later become my passion.

Suddenly I found myself immersed in an entirely different realm of health care than I had previously experienced. I went to educational conferences and learned from leaders in the fields of hormone health, stress management, mindset, and nutritional management. I saw pharmacy owners implementing these practices in their businesses alongside medical professionals who supported their endeavors. Furthermore, I was truly experiencing "health" care implementation instead of traditional medicine's "disease" care protocols.

Finally, I knew I was right where I needed to be! I was experiencing a professional transformation that directly connected my heart to my education. This was going to be fulfilling, but I later learned that it wasn't going to be easy. I knew I was going to have to put in a lot of hard work to make my passion align with my career, but I also knew it was all going to be worth it.

As the years went on, I spent more time with premenopausal and postmenopausal women. I started to realize that these women were teaching me as much, or more, than I had taught them. Their wins and failures, life lessons about health, and stories about their relationships had impressed upon me so many values. Most importantly, I had learned that taking care of myself early and regularly, would pay off immensely as I transitioned into my later hormonally changing years.

The experiences I had with these women taught me about functional medicine before I knew what this term was. They taught me the power of mindset, rest, self-care, nutrition, exercise, and connection. Some of them had struggled significantly over the years and were paying for it with their hormonal health. Others had the fortune to care for themselves and were living active, energetic lives well into their senior years.

I was driven to learn more, apply more, and teach more about the knowledge I was acquiring. I felt so fortunate to have this incredible opportunity to teach others and continue to learn myself. With each new patient, every specialty conference, and each diagnostic test, I was gaining knowledge that I knew had to be shared with my sisters everywhere. This was an often overlooked area that affects every single woman's life. It was clear someone needed to step up and start talking about preventative care and hormones to avoid the potentially devastating and debilitating health outcomes. I was, and still am, determined to be that person.

The first step towards bringing the change that the women of the world need, isn't necessarily going to be found just through sharing my personal story. It will however be found in the stories, experiences, science, and gifts that need to be passed on to women who are approaching their hormonally changing years. For those who have already gone through the "change", I believe these same stories and gifts will add tremendous value to your lives as well. A combination of my story with the stories of others is how I plan to empower women to embrace and nurture their health so they can thrive for years and years to come. I want women to feel empowered by aging and feel strong, sexy, informed, and vibrant!

Since the beginning, I've grown up as the daughter of a Pharmacist. I learned quickly that there was a pill, suspension, or diagnosis for everything. I was raised with a constant supply of vitamins, antibiotics, tablets, and cough medicine. My amazing father, the Pharmacist, used medical terms around the house to be both silly and educational, such as "pass the sodium chloride" or "brush your teeth before you get trench mouth." This naturally propelled my interest in the sciences.

My Dad was an OG Pharmacist. An original. A class act. This also meant he was a hard worker, came home late, and was exhausted most of the time. He owned his own Pharmacy and taught me the value of dedication, customer relations, and kindness. He knew most of his patients by name, accepted trades as payment, hand-delivered medications, educated his patients, supported his employees' personal development, and went above and beyond to support the needs of the business. I remember as a child going on late night hospice calls with him and my family, sometimes driving an hour each way just to deliver medicine. I also distinctly recall my Dad complaining about declining reimbursement before I ever knew what an "Average Wholesale Price", was.

At the university level, I majored in biochemistry and took my first job at a hospital pharmacy as a technician when I was 18 years old. The excitement of taking college courses at the medical school and working alongside many healthcare professionals both inspired and intimidated me. I had a memorable group of classmates that pushed each other to excel with each exam, lab, and lecture. We were competitive with each other, but in a positive way. I couldn't thank them enough for the comradery and dedication that we developed while working towards being our best and fostering the drive to succeed.

When my education started to progress and I was accepted into pharmacy school, I thought I had it all figured out! I would get my Doctorate, go back to my hometown, and work with my Dad in hopes of taking over his pharmacy. Oh, how I was wrong! Although pharmacy school was intense, it introduced me to many valuable ideas, professional niches, people, and dreams about what I could do with my education to achieve financial freedom.

My Dad's brother, my Uncle, was also a Pharmacist. As immigrants to the United States, they learned about hard work and sacrifice from their parents, so enrolling in pharmacy school was hope for a secure future. I chose to go to the same university as they did and was very proud to share in their legacy. I walked the halls with the Assistant Dean and showed him their photos. I ate in the same student union building as they did and eventually went into an independent retail pharmacy just like them. They also both owned their own pharmacies. I had it in my blood to own my own business, someday.

Between my lifelong exposure to science, the competitive nature of my college classmates, my pharmacy school's dedication to education, and my family history, I was destined to want more from my career and the opportunities it would hold. I wanted my career to align with my passions in a way that would bring joy and healing into the lives of those around me. I was determined to make it happen, one way or another.

My professional career evolved through many areas of pharmacy practice. I was a Pharmacist for a retail chain, home infusion pharmacy, small-town hospital pharmacy, and multiple independently owned retail pharmacies. I was concerned that having too many jobs over the years would harm my ability to be hired, but it turns out it just made me a well-rounded pharmacist.

Once my career started taking off as a compounding pharmacist in 2006, I found myself immersed in a world of bio-identical hormones, adrenal care, thyroid function, gut health, and the intertwining dance that tie these together. The basic concepts of hormones make perfect sense to me, but the practitioners I worked with were not being taught about them and clearly needed help. Let me restate that, the practitioners were taught the basics of hormone physiology but they were not taught how to treat hormonal decline with much more than manufactured, brand named medications that were marketed to them.

This pharmacy was unique in that it was designed to allow for extended patient consultations and diagnostic testing. I was able to develop important relationships based on trust and was encouraged by the owners to grow the hormone and supplement area of the business. I may not have been working with my Dad, but I had an innate knowledge of how to care for the patient and dedicate my efforts and loyalty to the growth of the business. I was proud of what I did, how I did it, and what I stood for. I was respected and thanked for the role I played in this family business, although it wasn't *my* family.

My exposure to the basic building blocks of health kept showing up in many areas of my profession, yet very few people seemed to be practicing with those same basics. I was determined to help more practitioners and patients open their minds about replacing the body with what it was missing, instead of covering up a diagnosis with a band-aid. Thankfully, a handful of these practitioners regularly reached out to me for help when their patients required another form of care. My life seemed pretty textbook until a bomb dropped.

My mom was at lunch with a friend when she suddenly experienced extreme nausea before eating her meal. This lifesaving friend recognized that something bigger was happening. She rushed my mom to urgent care, where she was shocked to learn that she was having a heart attack! After an ambulance ride and a series of tests, she was rushed into surgery, resulting in a triple bypass. I was so thankful for her positive outcome, but I was confused. Why, did a seemingly healthy woman, have no idea she was in such a dire state?

My preventative brain started to spin. Do I now have a history of heart disease in my family? I needed to make sense of her health situation, so I started asking her long-term health questions. I also performed some tests and was on a search for answers. It turns out that my mom had lived a life of chronic inflammation that was further exacerbated by her diet, prior smoking history, and use of unopposed estrogens. She was doing everything that society and medicine had told her to do in the 80s and 90s but ultimately it worked against her. The takeaway was not that I had a family history of heart disease, but that lifestyle, medications, and dietary issues contributed to her increased risk of developing heart disease.

Our bodies have the ability to turn on or off certain genes based on how we live our lives. The food we feed it, the environment we expose it to, and the nutrients we provide or deplete it of, are all life-altering decisions we have to make each and every day. My Mom was living a clean life but was unaware that her past had increased her risks for illness and no one had ever mentioned that to her before. I am proud to say that she now regularly goes to the gym, avoids inflammatory foods, and lives a healthier life than she ever has before. She maintains her appointments with her traditional doctors but now she has me, her personal health advocate, to help guide her in her health journey towards complete and total healing.

Over the years, I have gained experience, education, and practical exposure to the world of functional medicine. Oddly, I hadn't applied that term "functional medicine" to what I was doing yet. I did, however, feel like an anomaly in my area of expertise. I found myself constantly recommending and defending the basics of nutrient replacement, adrenal care, gut health, and hormone balancing to an audience that had not learned of their importance.

Then finally, the concept of functional medicine was introduced to me at a conference in 2017. I was attending the *American Academy of Anti-Aging Medicine* Conference. At the time, I was working for another independent pharmacy that recognized the value of integrative medicine and encouraged me to learn and educate our patients by offering thorough consultations. I had found the space, colleagues, and science that I needed to support the area of medicine that nurtured my soul. This was truly the beginning of my career expansion towards a whole-body focus on health, and the fire in me began blazing!

Today, I am an advocate of using lifestyle, food, and supplements as a means to turn off the bad genes that we are given and accentuate the good genes that we have in order to live a longer, healthier life. Years ago, I decided that I had to find a way to help women learn that there is a better way to age with energy, strength, and exuberance. Women need to know that they can feel more hormonally balanced and that menopause doesn't have to be a sentence that ends with a period!

Being employed behind the counter as a pharmacist does not allow me the platform, or time necessary, to educate women the way I've felt most called towards. With this in mind, I furthered my education and created my own functional medicine business. The reason I have made this decision is to spend more time with my clients and better educate them on ways to conquer hormonal changes, manage their stress, and thrive during their transitioning years.

Now, as a Certified Functional Medicine Specialist™, I finally have the platform to share my voice. By regularly sharing my knowledge truth bombs, allowing my audience to know and trust me, creating programs, and developing webinars, I will better be able to reach those women out there that didn't even know that there is a better way to live. I feel that as humans, we can complicate situations but I am here to make the journey more simple so that we can all grow up feeling healthy, vibrant, and sexy.

It took me 23 years in my professional career to finally say I am a business owner like my Dad and Uncle. I moved through a lot of different pharmacy philosophies and niches to get to where I am today. I still love the intensity of working in a pharmacy and helping people, but I truly love working with clients on a deeper level, in the timeframe I see fit, to make a bigger impact in their life.

Health is something to be valued, and you have so much control over your health outcomes. But if you don't know where to look or which small symptoms could be a clue to a larger problem, then you are missing out, and I'm so glad you are reading this book. I want to educate and help people recognize their options through stories, experiences, science, and conversation.

Regarding the hormonal transition, I believe premenopausal, menopausal, and postmenopausal women are beautiful and strong. They are powerful, capable, wise, and adventurous! Every woman, if given enough time, will experience menopause and can live many valuable years beyond that transition. I vow to empower busy women to say goodbye to overwhelm, exhaustion, hormonal imbalance, and weight gain and achieve sustainable energy, whole-body balance, and effortless weight loss. I am passionate about helping women understand why and how caring for themselves now will help them to create a more fabulous future! It is possible, and I am here to empower you to make this your reality.

ABOUT DR. KELLYE SCHAB

Dr. Kellye Schab is a Certified Functional Medicine Specialist™ from The STORRIE™ Institute, owner of *Balanced Wellness*, Doctor of Pharmacy, author, educator, speaker, patient advocate, hormone health expert, and Compounding Pharmacist. Dr. Kellye has improved lives working with aging women for 20+ years while managing her own hormonal challenges and that of her three daughters. Upon learning that her own health was in peril at the age of 36, she vowed to focus on women's health in an effort to improve her own hormonal outcome and for the future lives of women everywhere.

Her expertise includes a feature in Authority Magazine, a continuing education lecture, contributor to a web-based menopause platform, and as a virtual summit speaker.

Dr. Kellye empowers busy women to say goodbye to overwhelm, exhaustion, hormone imbalance and weight gain to achieve sustainable energy, whole-body balance, and effortless weight loss. She is passionate about helping women understand the why's and how's of caring for themselves to make their hormonally aging transition less daunting and for a more fabulous future.

www.drkellyeschab.com | connect@drkellyeschab.com | LinkedIn: @drkellyeschab

Chapter 10

WHEN YOU KNOW IT'S TIME FOR CHANGE

By: Dr. Kourtney Powers, PharmD, CFMS

You will never be able to escape from your heart.
So it is better to listen to what it has to say."
– PAULO COEHLO "THE ALCHEMIST"

It was over 16 years ago, but I remember walking out of my last clinical rotation of pharmacy school like it was yesterday! The sun was shining, it was a beautiful Spring day. I had just turned 25 years old, and I felt like I had the world in the palm of my hand. I was about to graduate from pharmacy school with my PharmD, and I couldn't wait to drop all of this awesome knowledge on anyone and everyone looking to achieve wellness and improve the quality of their lives! Little did I know that I was about to enter into the corporate world of overbearing compliance of policies and procedures, where pharmacists are forced to worry more about the net worth of billion-dollar companies, rather than using their clinical knowledge and education to practice patient care and improve the lives of others. It wasn't until about ten years later that my "real" career began.

In complete transparency, I had struggled in my position as a retail pharmacist for quite some time. I had just graduated with my Doctorate in Pharmacy, but I wasn't even applying most of this clinical knowledge that I had just obtained. I worked for a corporate giant and each day was more miserable than the next. I made decisions based on corporate policy, not based on the benefit of my patients. I felt like a robot. I couldn't be myself, I was always acting as a representative of this corporation. Even the thermostat controlling the temperature in my store in Pennsylvania was controlled by company headquarters, five states away! There were so many other areas of pharmacy that I could switch to, but I always felt inclined to be on the forefront, communicating with patients and truly helping them and their loved ones. It is so much more than a "job" when you help a frazzled parent with their sick child or speak with, and reassure heart-broken family members with some guidance, support, and genuine care, who are coming in to pick up end-of-life hospice medications knowing there is not much time left for them to be with their loved one. I know it is truly my calling to work directly with patients needing my empathy, compassion, kindness, and knowledge in order to help them navigate their health and wellness.

This patient interaction reflects my personality, my passion, and my purpose in my field, and I couldn't imagine doing anything different. But that wasn't what it was all about. I spent my days wrapped up in insurance issues and trying to keep up for 14-hour shifts that were understaffed due to corporate cutbacks. I mean, to the point of actually getting a UTI because there was just no time to run to the bathroom. Yeah, that actually happened to me, and I'm sure a lot of other dedicated pharmacists or healthcare professionals have fallen victim to this as well. It was a terrible quality of life for me, and it is the story of most retail pharmacists across the board. It's like being human isn't an option, constantly being pushed to your limits, seeing how much you can endure both physically and mentally is the norm. You can't have a bad day, because that bad day can cause you to make an error or bypass something important, and people are always relying on us. The field of pharmacy still remains as "America's most trusted profession."

It wasn't until I became pregnant with my son that I realized this wasn't a healthy way to live. It wasn't just about me anymore and what I could endure during a 14-hour shift. I was "lucky" enough to obtain a job with another corporate giant, but this was for mail order. I was able to work from home and have a flexible schedule, as I was expecting my son to arrive in just a few short months. It wasn't my dream pharmacy job, but I was able to balance my career, use the degree that I worked so hard to achieve, and be a stay-at-home mom. I felt blessed that this was an option. However, this job brought an entirely new level of burn-out rate regulations, as I was required to verify a minimum of 192 prescriptions per hour and for eight hours a day. Imagine that! There were times I would work in different departments where I was able to reach out to patients and doctors, which made my job so much better because at least I was having contact with people. It just depended on where they needed help in the workflow. It was a rollercoaster ride, for sure. But I won't complain. I was able to be at home with my son, Christopher, until he was in school full-time. At this point, however, I was really itching for more in my career and knew that I needed a change. I wanted to practice pharmacy at the level of patient care. I wanted to interact with people and help them achieve wellness. I wanted more.

In my decision to look for a change, I found a new work home at a small, family-owned independent pharmacy through a mutual colleague. I didn't know anything about this pharmacy or this town that was almost an hour away from home, but what I did know was that a change was necessary. I needed an opportunity to do what I set out to do, to truly help people find healing. It was important to me to change people's lives for the better, helping them prevent illness and feel good physically and mentally. I was apprehensive about working so far from home and in a town that I was unfamiliar with, but I did it anyway. I would drive past a ton of chain pharmacies on my way to work every day, but I wouldn't have it any other way! This opportunity changed me, and changed the way I now practice pharmacy!

This new path of practice that I was headed down was pretty incredible. It took me a little while to shake the corporate policies out of me and learn to just do what I know and let my personality intertwine with my knowledge, drive, and compassion to help others. David, the owner of the pharmacy, would always laugh when I would ask the ever-present question, "Is it ok to do this? I don't remember anymore if it is the law or just a corporate policy." I was there for a few months and David asked me to step outside for a minute. I was like, "Oh crap! What did I do?" We went outside and he said, "Nice job, I knew you had it in you!" He noticed the shift in my practice, he saw my potential. I knew that I was finally in the right place to use my skills and thrive!

What I have learned over the past 16 plus years, is that so many doctors and patients are equally dissatisfied with the healthcare that they provide or receive within the system. I cannot count the patients that come to the pharmacy feeling lost after their doctor appointments, looking for answers, reluctant to start medications that were prescribed, and not even understanding why they were given a prescription, how it works on the body, and why this would "fix" their ailment. On the same note, I have spoken to so many wonderful doctors, PAs, and CRNPs who also feel they don't have enough time with their patients due to insurance mandates and back-to-back scheduling. The most important component of this "healthcare" interaction is an individual's understanding of their own health, how to stay healthy, and avoid illness and disease. In the current hamster wheel cycle, there is a minimal explanation of medications, interactions with their current medication regimen, what to expect as results, what side effects to expect, or the fact of drug depletion and replenishment to keep the body balanced. For every action on the body, there is always a reaction. But, most importantly, there is the missing component of nutrition, self-care, sleep, and holistic health practices that most physicians don't incorporate in their practice. They simply do not have the time.

My integrative practice really became present and known in the community almost six years ago when I stumbled upon CBD. We had some CBD oil samples and literature in the store that David had brought back from a pharmacy convention, and I was intrigued by what benefits it offered, as there was buzz that it was the next big thing for pharmacists to incorporate into their practice. I was curious about the information presented and how these products could help improve so many conditions. I had no idea about the legality of these products and how they differed from medicinal marijuana, another topic I knew pretty much nothing about at that time. What I did know was that marijuana contains THC, a schedule I drug, and it was illegal on the federal level to dispense as a pharmacist. I was fascinated, and so my CBD discovery journey began.

I dove in headfirst, researching all that I could about the cannabis plant. It was difficult to find a lot of information six years ago, as CBD had not become the common household name that it is now. What I had learned is that a professional-grade full-spectrum CBD tincture can be just as beneficial (or more) to a patient with certain qualifying conditions, making them eligible for a letter of recommendation for medicinal marijuana. The over-the-counter CBD tinctures that I recommend to my clients can work just as well as medical marijuana. Medical marijuana requires a letter from a doctor with a diagnosis for one of the legally approved uses and requires going to a dispensary, a facility, only for its distribution. I was curious and wanted to try the tincture for my own anxiety issues. I had suffered from general anxiety from my early 20s and would have random anxiety and quick little panic attacks throughout the day. Many times, my hands and feet would go numb, I'd have heart palpitations, and would become short of breath. This started happening several times a day and began interfering with my lifestyle and eventually caused me to seek medical attention. I was prescribed an ever-so-popular SSRI (selective serotonin reuptake inhibitor), which became the only way to completely stop the panic attacks. I was taking an antidepressant, but I didn't even feel depressed! I was on an SSRI for over 16 years, except for when I was trying to become pregnant, until a few months after my son was born when I was driving with him in the car and that awful feeling came over me. Fast-forward eight years, I introduced CBD into my daily regimen. In one week of using the tincture, I tapered myself off of the medication and have never looked back. Has it cured my anxiety completely? Nope! I take my CBD tincture every day, along with yoga, meditation, and breathwork, and I am a work in progress. But the good news is that my anxiety is under control so that I feel content and healthy throughout my day.

Throughout my research, the use of different products with myself and others, and through trial and error, I began teaching a class, "Let's Talk Hemp" several times a month. The class was always packed with people wanting to learn more about CBD and how it could help them. I started working with people one-on-one every day, talking about their health issues and figuring out therapeutic dosing that benefited their individual health concerns. I have watched first-hand as people transform their lives through their health, and as they have shared and continue to share their feedback and results with me. At this point, I have collected hundreds of written testimonials from grateful clients who are telling their stories of how happy they are with their life-changing results.

When I started down this path of healing and nurturing my patients, the one-on-one contact with them organically turned into more than just educating and guiding them through using CBD products. I got to know many of my clients on a personal level. I learned about them, their families, their lifestyle, their jobs, and their overall health. It was through the understanding of this big picture that my passion is fueled every day, as I continue to work with more clients. I guide them on a journey of healing and overall well-being, not just through the use of CBD, but through lifestyle modifications, supplements and nutrition, and most importantly getting to the root cause and solving medical issues from the source.

When I started down this path of researching cannabis and helping others, I never realized how it would completely change my practice as a pharmacist and lead me down this path that fills my heart with immense joy. I decided to take my education further and earned my Certification as an Integrative Nutrition Health Coach from the Institute of Integrative Nutrition (IIN). This institution is founded and directed by Joshua Rosenthal, whose mission is to enrich his students' lives, by teaching a "whole-life approach to health and happiness" by creating a balance of components that nourish us both on and off of our plates. There is no one-size-fits-all diet, and we must incorporate nutrition and personal growth to truly live fulfilling lives. While there is a time and a place for Western medicine, the curriculum from IIN sparked my interest even further to continue learning about non-traditional medical treatments. I learned about less invasive interventions such as using nutrition as medicine and maintaining health through lifestyle choices, exercise, stress management, and emotional well-being.

As I decided to continue in my quest for more knowledge about this practice, I was led to another opportunity to earn my certification as a Functional Medicine Specialist through the Functional Medicine Business Academy, founded by Dr. Christine Manukyan. This discovery changed my life and pivoted the focus of my practice. I stumbled upon Dr. Christine's story on social media, as she posted a quote from Paulo Coelho, who just happens to be the author of my favorite book. I read her story in her first best-selling book, "Pivot with Purpose," where I immediately thought to myself, "WOW! This feels like me speaking! She knows exactly how I feel! I need to talk to this woman!" We connected on a call and I decided to join her Academy. From day one of working with Christine, my life started to change. My practice, my mindset and my career quickly shifted. I am so lucky and blessed that a higher power crossed our paths and that I am now a part of this wonderful tribe of clinicians that she has compiled. God always has a plan.

It was important to me to incorporate mind, body, and spirit into my practice, as I have always enjoyed my own personal yoga and meditation practices. I completed my yoga instructor certification through a yoga and self-awakening program created and taught by Theresa Moore, LMT at her wellness center, *Peaceful Journeys*. I also became a certified Reiki Practitioner and learned many holistic therapies to share with my clients through this program, including bach flower therapy, foot reflexology, ear candling, raindrop therapy, crystal energy healing, chakra balancing, restorative meditation, mala meditation, breathwork, herbal therapy, aromatherapy and the many uses of essential oils. Not only have I used all of these incredible practices on myself, but I also love to share them with my clients, who are able to benefit from them as well! I am so blessed to have Theresa, another wonderful soul, in my life! Not only is Theresa one of my dearest friends, but she has also taught me so much holistically and spiritually from her own natural lifestyle. She has proved to me that mindset and gratitude are the keys to everything and is consistently teaching everyone in her sphere how to live a happy, balanced life.

In the midst of receiving all of this education and guidance, *Balanced Wellness Solutions*, my functional/integrative medicine practice was born. I spent my free time working with clients in my own practice, doing what I love. All of these life transformations happened in the order that God intended for me to understand, plan, and transform my own life and my practice as a clinician. I now have the opportunity to walk in my calling to help others find real solutions and live the balanced life that we all deserve to live.

Entering into this practice of functional medicine is so important to me because it aligns with my ethics, encouraging more effort on disease prevention instead of waiting to treat a disease once it manifests. The incidences of heart disease, diabetes, and cancer, just to name a few, could be significantly reduced just by making better lifestyle choices. I am passionate about my philosophy of combining my experience, knowledge, and understanding of my patient's needs in order to balance the mind, body, and spirit. In my time with them, we address the root causes of their symptoms and illnesses resulting in disease prevention, the ability to slow down the progression of a disease, or even reverse the condition altogether.

As a Functional Medicine Practitioner, I not only focus on the underlying, root cause of a health condition, I practice relationship-centered care, taking the time to listen to my clients, with a deep understanding that every person is a bioindividual. There is no cookie-cutter answer to each person's unique characteristics and health background. I use my empathy, compassion, and understanding to help integrate the best therapy for each individual, working with them in collaboration to set and achieve goals. We are partners. They are responsible for their own actions towards achieving complete health, and I act as an educator, a role model, and a mentor to them. It is so important to realize that implementing this form of healthcare creates a crusade for wellness and prevention, having the potential to change the trajectory of people's lives, including my own.

In my current practice as a clinician, and through being in contact with a variety of people on a daily basis, I have noticed that so many people are struggling with anxiety, depression, and stress. People are often feeling overwhelmed by living in the fast-paced times of technology and an "I want it now" society. Not to mention the addition of the daily covid-related mayhem we've been experiencing for over 2 years now. Fortunately and unfortunately, people are taking a lot of medication to help cope with the turbulence of the times, navigating through to the best of their abilities. Technology increases on the daily, and everything and everyone seems to be moving faster than ever. So many of my clients voice their frustration and sadness over their inability to keep up with their demanding schedules, as well as that of their families and friends. They feel as though they are unable to enjoy the fun times or are missing the small details in life. They no longer enjoy the gifts through the surrounding nature as they are always preoccupied with the ever-present noise and the hectic hustle and bustle of keeping up with the responsibilities, requirements, and expectations of life. These distractions have changed us as a society and culture and yet, we continue to evolve. This stress is real and it affects our health more than we realize.

I am often guilty of this hectic, fast-paced lifestyle, myself. I am constantly playing a balancing game in my job at the pharmacy, in my functional medicine practice, and in my personal and family life. I found myself in this tapped-out position, realizing that I was in the relatively same physical and emotional position that I was in many years ago. In November 2021, I decided to take a few steps back. There is never a perfect time for change, but I knew down to my core that it was time for me to take back my life.

Covid has been both a challenge and a blessing, changing so many people's lives, both positively and negatively. I was working in an environment that had changed so much, it was starting to change me. I was feeling overwhelmed and I just didn't have the time to work one-on-one with patients anymore. I was in an environment that was depleting me, both in and out of the workplace.

Change looked different for me this time. Instead of finding another pharmacy to work for, I made the decision to cut my hours back in the pharmacy drastically in order to fulfill my passion and my purpose in the functional medicine space. I began working more intentionally with my clients. Covid not only changed my health and well-being, but I witnessed it change that of so many people individually, as well as our society as a whole. In addition, it truly spiraled traditional healthcare to an entirely new level of despair. These changes have made the need for functional medicine clearer than ever. Many people now realize that they need clinicians who can spend time with them to help overcome any concerns with their physical, emotional, and mental well-being. People need practitioners that will listen and take the time to get to the root cause. This is where I can intervene and help!

My journey has led me right here, right now, for a very specific reason. It is my lifelong mission to serve others and help them to achieve a life free from the stress and chaos of navigating the downfalls of Western medicine. I am on a mission to not only help people heal their bodies from within, but to walk with them as they create a life that they are proud of and feel good about. I am beyond excited to continue working with all of these dedicated people, who are looking for a change and are willing and committed to their health. It is a joy in my life to have the opportunity to help people achieve their goals of living a happy, healthy, and fulfilling life. It really is possible, and I am committed to making it my client's reality.

> *"One day you will wake up and there won't be any more time to do the things you've always wanted. Do it now."*
>
> – Paulo Coehlo

ABOUT DR. KOURTNEY POWERS

D r. Kourtney Powers is a Certified Functional Medicine Specialist™-from The STORRIE™ Institute, Certified Integrative Nutrition Health Coach from the Institute of Integrative Nutrition, Certified Yoga Instructor and Reiki Practitioner, and a CBD specialist, certified in Medicinal Cannabis Education in the state of Pennsylvania. Dr. Kourtney is the CEO and founder of her Functional Medicine Practice, *Balanced Wellness Solutions, LLC* as well as hosts the *Balanced Wellness Solutions Podcast.*

Dr. Kourtney is passionate about providing education and support through her group, "Let's Talk Hemp with Kourtney." Her true passion is educating people on the use of CBD and helping them navigate many health conditions. She has helped hundreds of people transform their quality of life using CBD and continues her work each day.

Working in a retail setting for over 16 years as a pharmacist, Dr. Kourtney recognized that there must be a better alternative for people taking so many prescriptions and still not feeling well. Always looking for natural and holistic therapies for herself and others interested in a different approach to health and wellness, she experimented on herself, when she substituted her 16-year prescription medication with a plant. It worked! This sparked a newfound love of holistic therapy that she continues to embrace and share with her clients today.

In her hybrid virtual and in-person practice, Dr. Kourtney's purpose and passion is to continue to help people seeking alternatives to Western Medicine when they are really looking for the "why" they have an illness and helping them get to the root cause. She helps her clients achieve health and wellness through living a healthy lifestyle, focusing on nutrition, gut health, crushing anxiety, using CBD, hormone balancing, movement, mindset, focus, supplements, self-care, and helping people achieve balance through nourishment both on and off their plates.

www.wellness-solutions.co | dr.kourtney.sanfelice@gmail.com |
IG: @dr.kourtney.sanfelice |
Podcast: Balanced Wellness Solutions with Kourtney

Chapter 11

EVOLUTION OF INTEGRATIVE HEALING

By: Lusine Chorekchyan, NP, CFMS

"Stop asking people for directions to places they've never been."
– GLENNON DOYLE

What does the concept of being "healthy" mean for you? Does it mean the same thing as feeling alive? Maybe it means having a zest for life and remaining passionate? Does it mean enjoying your existence and thriving? Whatever it means to you, the truth is that health doesn't start and end with just a yearly primary care check-up. Health is much more dynamic and three-dimensional than what it has been reduced to. Now more than ever we are seeing all the holes and failures emerge in our conventional medical system. As the world speeds up and becomes more complex, the need to connect with our core and prioritize our health becomes exceedingly necessary. Compared to centuries past, we seem to be living longer as a population with higher standards of living but a lower quality of life, leading to less whole-life satisfaction. As the demands of the world increase, our essence seems to slowly fade into the background. Health and wellness are far too often overlooked, and now is the time to redefine them.

When I began my career as a family nurse practitioner back in 2014, I was so excited to go out there and start changing lives by helping patients improve their health. I was full of passion for health and wellness and was convinced my studies had equipped me with the knowledge to find the answers to all ailments. I understood that I needed the experience to perfect the art of medicine, but was convinced that with time and practice there would be no ailment that I could not help to improve. My studies in graduate school implied that conventional medicine had all the answers and I was an agent of conventional medicine ready to grace my patients with healing. Looking back, I realize it was naive and arrogant to think that our current system was somehow ideal. However, that was the culture that I was indoctrinated with during university, that is the underlying belief and culture of the conventional western medical model. With time, I became tired of prescribing medication to my patients that would address surface-level symptoms, rather than the root cause of their pain or illness. I was starting to feel frustrated that the intention I began with, to bring health and wellbeing to those I served, was not possible because there was no time or space to look at the whole being. All too often the systems in place were disempowering to the health seeker and enabling of his or her dependence on pills for a quick solution, an ephemeral fix. Looking back now, I wish I could tell my younger self all the ways that conventional medicine in the insurance-paid world is limiting. My intention is not to devalue conventional western medicine, but to open dialogue and allow for an objective understanding of where its values lie and where it needs to evolve. I am grateful however for the experiences I've had in the standard medical world. It has helped me identify all the ways the existing system works, as well as the ways it requires modification and supplementation. The value of conventional western medicine can be upgraded by integrating other modalities of healing for a more holistic approach.

Whether I am in my role as a primary healthcare provider, am the patient, or am the loved one of a health seeker, I am tired of treating the symptoms instead of the cause. The understanding of health and wellness is so much more than what it has been reduced to. Instead of looking at human beings as a large masterpiece of intricate functioning and tangible experiences, our current system focuses on reducing us to compartmentalized pieces of flesh that function together to compose a human. This is dehumanization at its core. Unfortunately, patients are sometimes seen as flesh instead of complex human beings. Quite often the ailment of the "flesh" in question, succumbs to the redundant and irresolute consumption of pills, all with the hopes that it will solve a problem that, in time, putrefies the flesh it was meant to preserve. In other words, the pills we are prescribing are frequently doing more harm than good. Don't get me wrong, these chemical concoctions aren't short of magic as they do save lives and solve immediate problems, but is that enough? What about increasing the overall quality of life? Conventional medicine has done many wonderful things, but it has not addressed many of the most important aspects of health and wellness and rarely identifies the root causes, which is the most important part of improving one's quality of life.

In most cases and places, medicine is being practiced in a very prehistoric and exclusionary manner, prioritizing quantity over quality. We are yearning for an evolution in our healthcare system to pivot towards a holistic approach. We need to be treating the whole human and improving the human experience at its core. It is not about how well your heart or liver functions in a vacuum or as cells in a petri dish, but rather, it's about how well you thrive in life each and every day. Thriving physically, mentally, emotionally, and spiritually equates to an experience of health, vitality, and creativity. No matter how you want to pursue improving your health, the first step is to look within for the map and directions.

The universe or a higher power waits for you to align within yourself, then it aligns the stars to illuminate your path. That alignment process is not obvious at first, however. It's a preparatory state, a discovery state, an unfolding of sorts. As you grow and evolve, it will reveal itself to you. Often the most obvious point in this unfolding is quite unpleasant. It's a feeling of being out of place, a feeling of dissatisfaction, and a place of dissonance. Perhaps it's not of complete lack, but it is like a puzzle with multiple pieces missing. As you start, you create movement and are on a search to find what resonates with your new sense of self. As you continue to grow, the movement you have created pushes you to keep growing.

In time, my perspective on health has evolved and shifted. I have re-discovered the value of going back to the basics of health, and with it have learned the value of functional medicine as a major component of holistic modalities of care. I feel committed to integrating natural processes of healing with traditional approaches. In fact, I think they should be linked together, incorporated, and woven together into an all-encompassing tapestry, a warm blanket to cocoon the whole being, to treat the whole self. There is value in finding how the earth and nature, the food we eat, and our bodies innately, provide for the health and healing we need. In addition, there are less known and less utilized forms of healing with energy that ties in with the holistic method of approaching wellness. Energy healing has been utilized successfully for centuries, but only now is viewed through the lens of science. There are so many modalities that are either unacknowledged by the western medical community or are looked at as subordinate to the worldwide acceptance of conventional medicine. Although not all modalities of holistic healing have gone through the scrutiny of the scientific method, many have been placed under the scrutiny of time and centuries of documented experiences with positive outcomes. Often, the greatest discoveries are scrutinized until a time comes when science evolves enough to conduct the research studies and explain the findings in a scientific manner. Fortunately, functional medicine has been and continues to be based on robust research and is fully rooted in science. It endorses an individualized approach to health that is unique to the client and patient benefiting from the healing practice.

"Set your life on fire. Seek those who fan your flames."
– Rumi

Prior to delving into functional medicine, I started reading books about nutrition, fasting, plant medicine, energy medicine, and researching during my free time. I didn't start with a clear goal in mind, but rather due to a natural curiosity and drive. I felt like there was so much more out there to learn that was beyond what I had been exposed to in my medical education program. I wanted to find answers for my patients that I could not find through conventional medicine. Furthermore, I had been searching for schools and courses that would provide a structured and research-based curriculum that I could utilize in my practice, but I couldn't quite locate one that provided what I was looking for. I happened to discuss some of my ideas with a very close friend of mine, Armine Gukasyan, who mentioned that another friend of hers, also a nurse practitioner, was studying and practicing something called functional medicine. At the time, I didn't fully comprehend what it really meant to practice functional medicine, but nonetheless, a seed was planted within me. Quite coincidentally about a year after that initial conversation, right at the beginning of the 2020 pandemic when everything was falling apart in the world, another good friend of mine, Dr. Christine Manukyan, called me. She told me she was signing up for some functional medicine classes and asked if I wanted to join her. I thought it was a funny coincidence that now, a second friend was urging and mentioning functional medicine. Strangely enough, before I even investigated the classes the idea strongly resonated with me, and my instincts told me to go for it. This period of expansion was catalyzed by the planting of the seed that an alternative medical practice was available to me. My friends helped expedite my desire and search to evolve my view of what health and wellness meant and the way in which I should serve. It was also at a time of great uncertainty in the medical field. Related to the novel coronavirus, there was so much anxiety and a fervent search for answers occurring. I was desperately trying to find ways of boosting my immune system through supplements and other natural remedies in hopes of doing whatever I could on my part to help protect my loved ones and patients. At the start of the pandemic, I felt there was no better time to embark on a new journey of incorporating a new and improved way to heal and stay healthy. Functional medicine was the gateway that opened an opportunity for me to feel more liberal in incorporating energy medicine into my existing knowledge and skill base. This was the point at which I decided to start studying Reiki alongside the basics of functional medicine.

You may be asking, "Why Reiki? What is that?" Reiki is "an energy healing technique that promotes relaxation, reduces stress and anxiety through gentle touch. Reiki practitioners use their hands to deliver energy to your body, improving the flow and balance of your energy to support healing[1]." Now, let me tell you why *I* chose to start here. Years ago, after some personal life challenges, I decided to have a Reiki session to help with some tender loving care for my soul. I came out of that session feeling like my soul went to the spa. I had more clarity and tranquility and felt as if the concerns that were buzzing within my being, were finally settled, leaving a clear surface for me to build on.

Having practiced traditional medicine for many years, my experience provided the perfect launching point to start the journey of energy healing and functional medicine together. Both functional medicine and energy healing look at the root causes of a specific disease and offer treatment methods that are closer and more harmonious to the organic function of the body, mind, and soul. Functional medicine analyzes every aspect of a person's life and experiences, to find the connection between the disease states and the root causes. The purpose of functional medicine is to determine how the ailments can be treated using lifestyle modifications, supplementation, nutrition, and toxin reduction by using clean products in order to boost health outcomes. It utilizes a diagnostic approach that is not available at your regular doctor's office. It also uses special lab tests to dive deeper into the functioning of the body beyond the standard lab draw. Not only that, but it really focuses more on the root cause of an existent disease, as well as preventing the potential development of a disease.

"The secret of change is to focus all of your energy, not on fighting the old, but on building the new."

– SOCRATES

There is so much that affects a person's health and well-being. Let me explain further. Think about the array of things that impact your body, mind, and spirit. Think about the multitude of things you interact with on a regular basis. Everything, I mean everything, affects your well-being whether, in a positive or negative way, your body is affected by everything you put in or on it. My goal is to orchestrate a holistic approach utilizing functional medicine along with modalities of energy medicine. It is more about empowering a client and equipping them with tools to serve the individual for a lifetime. I want to transcend the concept of "becoming healthy" into becoming energetically, as well as physically, optimized healing beings in action. Healing is an ongoing process that continues to regenerate within a person, so that it may transform a person from living or existing to actually thriving. After all, as long you are breathing and alive you are guaranteed to have life experiences that are challenging and therefore health is not a means to an end but rather a daily goal. Heath is a way of being that requires a complete approach that addresses the whole person.

This realization inspired me to open my own practice called, *Integrative Innovative Holistics LLC (IIH)*. IIH is built upon my integrative knowledge of holistic medicine, through encompassing energy healing and functional medicine, to help my clients find whole-being healing. My aim is to serve patients and clients searching for answers to the root cause of their ailments. I will help develop personalized health plans and to coach clients back to exceptional health and well-being. Over the last many years of being in healthcare, I have come to realize that when treating a patient's condition, like diabetes, you are never just treating the patient's condition. Unfortunately, the conventional medical system is set up in a way that only allows for limited time and resources to be shared with a patient. Meanwhile, it isn't hard to see that the disease is really just a symptom of some kind of underlying cause. What about the individual's eating habits, mental and emotional state, literacy level, skill development? What makes the individual excited and eager? What about the specific chemical or DNA makeup of the individual and how that dictates predisposition to a disease state? What about how a particular individual's digestive system metabolizes micro and macronutrients? Clearly, diabetes is only one of many examples that I could address. Feel free to substitute it with any other diagnosis or chronic illness. There is so much more to look at when trying to identify the root causes of an illness. Within my functional medicine practice, I also am looking at radiation, electric, and magnetic pollution exposure. I'm considering the emotional abuse and generational trauma that someone may have experienced. Then I think about the chemical pollution our bodies are bombarded with every single day, in the air, in our food, in the hygiene and self-care products we use.

Do you see how complicated this is? Does it seem too complex? Impossible to tackle? With the way the conventional medical system is set up, absolutely it is! The patient is often unaware of the areas in their life that could be optimized. Having the right information is the answer to improving their health and wellbeing, however. People need to be provided with an individualized set of tools that allows them to be in the driver's seat towards taking back their health. They also need a practitioner who is willing to be a guide and supportive resource while they are on the road towards lifestyle rejuvenation. I am confident that I can integrate my background, knowledge, and experience in traditional medicine into my specialty and passion for functional medicine and Reiki. Merging my two worlds together is finally bringing real healing to the incredible people with whom I work alongside. My background as a primary care Nurse Practitioner puts me in a unique position to truly understand where clients are coming from and help them to fill in the gaps as to why certain symptoms have arisen.

In addition to, and not separate from the value and purpose of Reiki and functional medicine, there is so much out there that can be utilized to improve our wellbeing. I am a big proponent of exploring all the ways we can improve and better our health and the overall experience of being alive. There are other practices such as sound resonance healing, yoga, qigong, hypnosis, regression therapy, gratitude journaling, meditation, med beds, electromagnetic field therapy, color therapy, sacred geometry healing, the practice of grounding, crystal healing, aromatherapy, and I could go on and on. Then let's look at more clinical, and perhaps more advanced practices like measuring and interpreting detailed hormone levels and heavy metals in the body, calculating intake of phytonutrients and vitamins, incorporating epigenetic, and pharmacogenomics. Again, this is just a small snippet of what is out there in the world of functional medicine. There is endless knowledge and information out there that is still on the cutting edge of being recognized, and yet in the regular insurance-paid medical setting, we are still focused on the systemic approach to healthcare. We are using the same method and same treatments rooted in the same unilateral approach. What we have is fine, but it can (and should) evolve to be better, to be fantastic, even. I feel we must transcend this one-dimensional and linear way of approaching health. Sure, this is a complex system and perhaps change takes time, but we don't need to wait to put the wheels in motion. There is already so much that has been established but is underutilized and often goes unrecognized.

"How wonderful it is that nobody need wait a single moment before starting to improve the world."

– ANNE FRANK

This is a time of change, a shift from the old paradigm to the new. If you have an idea that you feel can help humanity emerge from the dark ages, this is your time to step forward and birth that idea into reality. So many people have brilliant ideas that lay dormant because they fear they don't have the skill, support, or finances to bring it to fruition. More often than not, however, it isn't the skill that is an issue because skills are learned through experience. You need direction and need to look for the right resources and support to bring about the ideas that form in the mind. As for finances, you'll be surprised at how small financial investments into your future can transform into larger sources of income, so long as you invest in the ideas that drive your passion and curiosity. I have seen and observed this phenomenon and I think it isn't so much about how much money you must invest in your dreams, rather how creative you can be and how open you will be to shifting your mindset from lack to abundance, from one source of income to multiple sources of income. It's a process of creation and imagination, and given the right guidance, you can create abundance for yourself as well. One of the key guiding figures in helping me step into my entrepreneurial role has been Dr. Christine Manukyan. She leads by example and practices what she preaches, meanwhile lending a helping hand to those looking for an avenue to expand their reality with their ideas. Although what she provides is geared towards clinicians creating and providing another avenue for healthcare and income, I think her methods can easily be applied to many forms of entrepreneurship.

True healing incorporates mental, emotional, and spiritual alignment along with one's physical health, which at its core translates to what frequency your being emits. It is about transcendence, both of the material and the immaterial self. Everything in this life and in our bodies, including our experiences and consciousness, is interconnected and so are you to everything that exists. In all areas of life, we must shift our thinking from a materialistic, black and white point of view, to one of boundless possibility. You must match your frequency with that of the desired outcome you want. With a change of mindset and actionable work, you will produce and bring forth your desired outcome. You must see yourself and feel as if you are already there, in that time and space you are currently manifesting. From that point, you start to vibrate closer in frequency to that of the reality you seek to create. The last step in this is taking action. One step after another, take action while maintaining that image and emotion of where you are heading. Of course, you can't forget about persistence! You are already capable enough, intelligent enough, and powerful enough to bring about the change and the inspiration you want to be materialized in the world.

> *"We are here to laugh at the odds and live our lives so well*
> *that Death will tremble to take us."*
> – CHARLES BUKOWSKI

The concept of health and well-being are constantly evolving, and we must contribute to this evolution as clinicians. Now more than ever, the well-being of people and their healthcare providers is in crisis. Healers and patients alike need options and new answers, and most of all they need new approaches to healing. The system in place is failing in many ways and will continue to fail us unless we contribute to its evolution by integrating a holistic approach and transforming our understanding of health. We must start incorporating the whole person and their journey towards wellness to reach a sustainable state of health. It is difficult to reach a state of optimized health without the recognition of a person's emotional, psychological, and physical experiences and dysfunctions. With the use of functional medicine and energy healing, we can provide a more holistic method of healing while helping patients develop lifestyle skills that can serve them for a lifetime. The concept of whole-being wellness should be a priority in medical care and health coaching. We already have illness care but we are lacking *effective* preventive care, which is an essential part of establishing a thriving society.

Reference:

1. *What is Reiki, and Does it Really Work?* (2021, November 18). Cleveland Clinic. https://health.clevelandclinic.org/reiki/

ABOUT LUSINE CHOREKCHYAN

Lusine Chorekchyan is a Board Certified Family Nurse Practitioner, a Certified Functional Medicine Specialist™ from The STORRIE™ Institute and a Master Level Certified Reiki Practitioner. Lusine is passionate about balancing traditional allopathic medicine with functional medicine and energy healing for a holistic approach to health and wellness. Lusine has spent over 8 years working in primary care, managing complex health conditions among vulnerable populations. Alongside work, she has been advancing into the fields of energy and functional medicine and launching her own practice, *Integrative Innovative Holistics, LLC (IIH)*. Her vision for *Integrative Innovative Holistics* is to offer functional medicine coaching as well as energy healing to her clients while in respect to their established standard medical care. She believes that the best medicine is one that integrates natural and holistic methods with that of standard medical practice.

After years in the medical field, Lusine began to see the cracks in the system where healthcare was falling short and patients were searching for other resources to help find an answer for their ailments. She became passionate about getting to the root cause of chronic disease and finding natural ways of approaching healing for long-term, high impact results. Her passion was born out of frustration from the limitations of standard medicine. She has always believed that to treat an ailment, you must treat the whole person and target the physical as well as the emotional or spiritual body of a person for true healing. She utilizes Reiki as a form of energy healing to target the emotional and energetic body, while using functional medicine to target the physical. She believes that the future of medicine and healing lie in breakthroughs in energy healing and advancements in functional medicine yet to come.

Lusine has been selected for a biographical publication by Marquis Who's Who in America as one of the top professionals in her field. She was also published in Authority Magazine for an article on the *Five Things We Must Do To Improve The US Healthcare System*. In 2021, Lusine was a guest speaker at the Functional Medicine Business Academy Summit, presenting holistic modalities of healthcare integration within allopathic medicine.

She remains passionate about innovation in healthcare by finding more natural and holistic approaches to help guide her clients towards long-lasting wellness.

www.lusinechorekchyan.com | Integ.Innov.Holistics@gmail.com
Instagram: @lusine.chorekchyan.np | LinkedIn: /lusine-chorekchyan
YouTube: Integrative Innovative Holistics with Lusine

Chapter 12

DARE TO DREAM

By: Dr. Mileta Kemeza, PharmD, CFMS

"The meaning of life is to find your gift.
The purpose of life is to give it away."

– WILLIAM SHAKESPEARE

I grew up in Lithuania, a small and beautiful country, whose history dates back thousands of years. Historians think that Lithuanians understood health as the second part of the soul. All healing information is passed on from generation to generation. Family members most often took care of the ill person before they asked for help from the healthcare providers. The most common method in traditional medicine healing was using medicinal plants. Lithuanians have been using this method for centuries to help heal our bodies from within.

During my childhood in Lithuania, I would often get sick. I had asthma at the time and that caused me to end up in the hospital frequently. I was, however, always being treated with natural remedies by my mother or grandmother first. Even after seeking a medical doctor's help, we would use many natural healing recommendations. All this to say, learning about a holistic approach to health-care started during my childhood.

After seeing multiple doctors, I realized that some of them were very caring and empathetic and their goal was to help their patients to truly heal faster. Others, however, would ignore the symptoms (even when you could hear me wheezing from outside the room) and did not care to help. The doctors that really cared, inspired me to be the very best healthcare practitioner possible, and care for my own patients in the way they did for me.

When I was a child, I knew that someday I would practice in the field of medicine. Growing up, I didn't view medicine as a profession, I felt it as my passion, my destiny, my way of living. Throughout my youth when receiving treatment in the hospital, I saw a lot of other suffering children. I understood what they were going through because I went through similar experiences. Those experiences allowed me to feel true empathy for people who were sick and suffering, and a strong desire to help relieve and restore the health struggles that so many people experience.

After graduating from high school in Lithuania, I started my healthcare journey by enrolling in nursing school to learn how to help the most vulnerable human beings. I learned about anatomy, psychology, treatment of different disease states, laboratory interpretations, taking care of trauma patients, and so much more. Not only was I learning, but I also had the opportunity to practice my skills, taking care of hospital patients and integrating my studies and experience. While caring for patients was fulfilling, I desired to know more and grow more as a clinician. I wanted to be able to evaluate patients and make independent decisions about their treatment plans.

After two years of studying in nursing school, our family was given a lifetime opportunity to come to the dream country, the United States of America. It happened because my grandfather had a lucky hand after filling out a lottery application for a green card. Needless to say, our family won that lottery and received a green card! I was beyond excited to come to the USA. I knew I would have the chance to explore new opportunities and reach my fearless dreams. Our whole family was excited, but at the same time nervous to leave our country. We were having to leave our loved ones and start to live a new life without knowing the culture or language very well at all. Since I was the oldest child, I was expected to assume all of the responsibilities and help our family with job searches and translating in every aspect of our day-to-day lives. It took an emotional toll on me and was extremely hard. Up until that point, I was used to my parents taking on the responsibilities, taking care of me, and speaking for me if needed. Suddenly, my whole world turned upside down, and I felt responsible for everyone else. It was a great challenge for me, but that experience made me stronger and more resilient in the end. I will always feel forever thankful for my parents who left their home, their parents, and their jobs in order for me and my sister to have a better future.

Even though it was hard to start a new life in a new country, I was determined that nothing would stop me from becoming a healthcare practitioner. I had to do some research to decide which area of healthcare I would like to pursue in this country. After researching extensively, I found out that there was a profession here in the United States that I had never heard of before in my country: clinical pharmacy. In Lithuania, a pharmacist's main role was to dispense medications and had nothing to do with the clinical side of care. After lots of hard work, energy, and enthusiasm, I started in pharmacy school at the University of Illinois in Chicago. During my clinical rotations, I felt most satisfied when I was able to help my sickest hospital patients with direct interactions. Being able to work with a whole healthcare team, review medications, educate about side effects and interactions, and connect with others as a trusted healthcare provider, made me most fulfilled. After graduating from pharmacy school, I decided to pursue a residency to prepare to work as a Clinical Pharmacist.

Ever since then, I have been on an exciting journey and have been working with some of the best clinicians in the country for over 17 years. Helping patients as a team by making sure they get the best treatment available and understand how to take care of themselves once they leave the hospital is a great joy to me. There was just one problem: there was no time to address the root cause of illness. There was no time to explore lifestyle choices and eating habits. After seeing the same patients coming back to the hospital, I felt that something was missing, and knew I could be doing more. I was able to help patients heal from acute problems, but patients with chronic medical conditions were not finding any real healing. Patient symptoms were being masked with medications and rarely did those symptoms ever truly resolve. I did not yet know that there was a better way to help patients...until the day I became the patient.

At one point in my career, my stress level had taken such a huge toll on my body and I physically could not handle it anymore. I thought to myself, "I am strong and will keep going no matter what." After all, I had three kids under the age of five, never had enough sleep, took care of patients and my own family, but in the midst of all that, I forgot that I needed to take care of myself. I was either pregnant or breastfeeding for the first 7 years of my kid's lives, and I never had enough sleep. Even if I slept 10 hours (which rarely happened), I would feel exhausted. I thought to myself, "I can just keep going without stopping and I'll be fine." I sure was wrong. I ended up in the hospital with bacteremia. Bacteremia is a bacterial infection in the blood. I felt so sick that I did not want to be in my own body anymore. Laying in the hospital bed and not being able to be with my family, made me rethink my entire life. I paused to look for answers on how I could possibly lead a healthier lifestyle so that this would never happen again.

I was talking with all the medical providers at the hospital, asking what I should do to prevent myself from getting sick again. Not even one of them was able to give me helpful advice. All I was told to do was finish the antibiotic course, continue living the way I did and just hope it would never happen again. It was then that I started to look for the root cause of my own health issues to figure out what I could do to feel energetic, healthy, and happy again. I started researching and I scheduled an appointment with a naturopathic doctor who spent over an hour listening to me, asking about my stressors, my diet, my habits, and then took a blood sample so that she could analyze it through the microscope herself. After the thorough health interview and assessment, she was able to give me practical advice. Not only did she talk to me about my diet and supplements I could start with, but she also taught me about the importance of practicing yoga and meditation in order to keep my stress level down.

This began my journey of figuring out how to live a truly healthy lifestyle and was also planting the seeds for my future in functional medicine. I learned that even if I exercise every day, eat balanced and nutritious foods, and take all the best supplements, that will surely help, but it is still not the full picture. If I continued to feel stressed out and didn't sleep well, I would still not be healthy or have energy. I had to address my body as a whole and not just by singular symptoms.

Several years after beginning my health journey, I discovered *The Wellness Way*, a wellness support group. I decided to do a 30-day no sugar challenge and was able to lose 20 pounds in one month and to this day, I have still kept it off. I was never able to lose weight after I had kids, even though I was eating seemingly healthy and balanced foods, like salads, fish, and fruits. I had never paid attention to the number of carbohydrates I was consuming though, and most importantly, I was not aware of when I was eating. Most of the time, I was just eating when I did not feel hungry. I would often eat when I felt stressed out as well. After the no sugar challenge, I learned to be very mindful about my eating and was always aware of when and what I was eating.

After I lost weight, I felt empowered and confident that I would be able to achieve anything I set my mind to achieve. I felt that my mind was in control of my body and not vice versa. I stopped eating emotionally, was conscious about the food I was eating, and able to control my food intake with my mindset. Losing that weight also helped me to feel confident, because I felt good and I looked good. I was not feeling frustrated anymore when I would put on my favorite dress. I did not have to avoid going to parties because of feeling like I had nothing to wear that made me feel beautiful. With great confidence came positive energy. While taking care of myself and my health, I was able to have more energy to take care of my family, my patients, and play with my kids.

Within my journey of reclaiming my health, I grew passionate about functional medicine. I understood that treating isolated symptoms will never solve the true cause of the problem. In order to find the solution, you have to understand what caused the problem in the first place and address those underlying issues. I believe that functional medicine is the future of medicine. The traditional healthcare model can still offer great value in treating acute cases, such as heart attacks, strokes, bacterial infections, or traumas, however, it is not resolving issues for patients with chronic conditions. It is important to spend time with each patient, listen to their story, get to know their lifestyle, their stressors, and their diets. Combining the information learned from a comprehensive health history intake, with specific lab tests, supplements, and a nutrition plan is truly the best way to help patients restore and revive their health.

I was also inspired to expand my knowledge of functional medicine and transform my approach to patient care, because of my oldest son. We found out that he has an innate weakness in the area of attention and executive functioning, which has caused a lot of stress for him at school and at home. The assignments that he was doing at home took him hours to complete. He would often go to bed at midnight because that's how long it would take him to finish the assignments. He would then be tired and nervous in the morning and would not be able to concentrate in class. It even got to the point that he would refuse to go to school and desperately did not want to live in that state of mind anymore. It was a vicious cycle. The whole family was affected and we were constantly trying to help him with organization, prioritizing, and managing his emotions. It was incredibly stressful dealing with the schools and making sure he got all the support needed in order to have equal access to learning. The whole process was quite overwhelming for all of our family. After trying medications to help with his focus and not being able to tolerate them due to harmful side effects, I sought alternative options. I discovered that functional medicine had the potential to help alleviate some of his problems as well. By completing specialized lab tests, taking specific supplements, altering his diet, and practicing mindfulness, he was finally able to overcome many of his setbacks.

As I walked through this with my son, I became an advocate for other parents who have experienced similar issues with their children. I continue to receive many questions from other parents, and I am glad to be able to help guide them through this process. My thorough approach supports parents and families as they navigate complex school considerations. It provides balance and gives them the tools and resources they need to help restore physical and emotional health for themselves and their loved one.

I share my story with you so that you can see how I was personally touched and able to heal through the power and beauty of functional medicine. I believe this realm of medicine offers true healing opportunities to real people, just like my son and I. After having this experience and seeing amazing results, I became passionate about helping others through using functional medicine principles. I could finally see a path towards a more meaningful and fulfilled life for myself. I wasn't quite sure what to do with my passion, however, and I did not know how or where to start. In 2021, my journey of discovering functional medicine, my life's passion, led me to Dr. Christine Manukyan. She was a gift sent by God. It was perfect timing. With her guidance, I was able to develop a clear vision of how I could become a functional medicine practitioner in the virtual space. Prior to meeting her, I never thought that as a pharmacist, I would be able to have my own virtual practice. I learned that I could start a business where I can help clients in their personal health journeys by taking the time to get to know them, ordering labs, creating personalized protocols and sending them professional-grade supplements and nutrition plans.

Each one of these incredible life experiences has led me here, to where I am today.

I am a Pharmacist, Certified Functional Medicine Specialist, and author. I had never even dared to dream about writing a book. Writing was always the hardest subject for me in school, as my essays were short and often lacked details. With the help of tutors, I was able to grow, improve and achieve straight A's, since anything else would have been below my expectations. I did it, but it took a lot of hard work and determination. Every area of my life in which I have been challenged to grow, has required of me to dream, stay committed and believe in what is possible.

I have worked hard to make the seemingly impossible possible, and I could not have done this without all of the people who have encouraged me along the way. I am so grateful to Dr. Christine Manukyan who has believed in me and has encouraged me to dream big. I have learned how to make my dreams a reality by taking massive action to change my life. If I had not made the decision to take back control of my life and health, I would not feel as though my mission on this planet would ever be complete. Functional medicine is the path that has allowed me to reclaim my life and fulfill my life's purpose. My encouragement to you is to dare to dream! And not only dream, but take action and make your dreams a reality. Do not wait to be perfect, because that can take a lifetime, and will likely still never happen. You do not want to waste the most precious gift you have on earth, your life. Start identifying your dreams now so you can have the rest of your life to make them your beautiful reality.

ABOUT DR. MILETA KEMEZA

D r. Mileta Kemeza is a residency-trained Clinical Pharmacist, Certified Functional Medicine Specialist™ from The STORRIE™ Institute, and a mother of three. She has worked in various hospital settings and clinics, collaborating with providers and helping hundreds of patients with chronic diseases optimize their medication regimens to achieve better health outcomes. Over the past 17 years, Dr. Kemeza has also helped to decrease hospitalizations and was recognized as a top patient educator and consultant to other medical professionals.

As a clinical pharmacist in the hospital setting, Dr. Mileta noticed the impact she had on patient care in the acute setting. She felt deeply connected to being able to help patients with acute illnesses, such as heart attacks, stroke, or infectious diseases, however, she understood that patients with chronic diseases, such as diabetes, hypertension, or obesity could greatly improve by utilizing a natural approach. This was the point at which she made the decision to help others identify the root causes of their diseases through practicing functional medicine.

Dr. Mileta Kemeza is passionate about helping exhausted moms of children with unique needs to transform their lifestyle with a functional medicine approach, to have more energy, less stress, and better sleep. Through identifying nutritional deficiencies and helping to develop a healthy mindset, she is able to guide her clients towards achieving positive results to reclaim their health and wellbeing. She believes that most chronic diseases can be reversed and health can be optimized using personalized testing to get to the root cause. She further customizes her framework for each individual, combining preventative lifestyle solutions and nutrition therapy.

drmiletakemeza.com | Facebook: /MiletaKemeza | Instagram: @mileta_pharmd

Chapter 13

THE QUEST FOR ABSOLUTE ANSWERS

By: Dr. Pana Ninan, PharmD, BS, CFMS

"What I know is, that if you do the work that you love,
and the work that fulfills you, the rest will come."

– Oprah Winfrey

To be completely honest, I feel like I was conned. I was told pharmacy was a great profession for women and working mothers. I was told there were jobs on every corner. I was told this was the most trusted profession in healthcare. These were all the things that made me feel like I would be taken care of, loved, and I would have an amazing career ahead.

I graduated in 2009, just after the big economic crash, and there were no jobs. I was so proud to have earned my doctoral degree and was ready to take on all the challenges that lie ahead. I had no clue what they would be, but I was up for it. I had worked hard to get through school and was excited to finally be able to work and make a living but companies were no longer expanding and pharmacists were not leaving their positions. Jobs were no longer available, especially full-time jobs near a big city like

Atlanta, Georgia. I was ready to establish my career and just needed to find a way to do so.

Upon graduation, I was able to secure a spot as a part-time floater, which meant they could not guarantee me hours, but if there was an opening anywhere in the district I could be called to help fill in. Since I was told my work shifts last minute, preplanning anything was impossible. This didn't suit me very well, so I worked hard to prove myself to my boss in order to earn a spot in a store as a full-time pharmacist. When that time came just a few short months later, I was given a store that was known as the worst in the district. I accepted the challenge unknowingly. This store had a clientele that was high maintenance. The store was very unorganized, the help was untrained, and the volume was high. I entered with enthusiasm about being a part of something, to have a partner and staff that would work together, and a community that would embrace me. Instead, it started with lots of inner store tension amongst the technicians, and I was hardly welcomed with open arms. I was constantly asked where the old pharmacist was and was often talked down to because I had not built rapport with them yet.

I worked my absolute hardest for 4 years to gain my community's trust, my technicians' respect, and my boss's approval. I worked 14 hours shifts with the gates open. I came in early to get a head start. I left late to clean up. I skipped meals to serve others. I never stopped. I didn't realize what I was doing to myself, though. I honestly, naively, thought this is what everyone did at work. This was what I signed up for when I chose to go to pharmacy school, so I now needed to rise up to the challenge.

My passion and excitement that I entered the profession with, moved on to stress and overwhelm. That overwhelm moved to exhaustion. I would wake up on my days off feeling as though I was hungover with bad headaches and was barely able to get out of bed. I felt so tired. It was not because of alcohol, but because of working two back to back 14+ hour shifts, not eating enough, and pushing myself to the max. I did that until one day before I gave birth to my first child. I worked like that until I was 40 weeks pregnant. When I had my first child, I was unknowingly in a state of burnout. As I look back now at the daily stress, the long hours, the tears, and the exhaustion, I now realize that was not normal. Once I left on maternity leave and had a moment to process all that happened, I knew I could not continue on that same path. It was time for something to change.

I ended up changing companies, not career paths, because I was labeled a "retail pharmacist" just because I did not complete a residency after school. I was thankful for the change of scenery, but then found myself back in the same situation. Since I was able to handle high volume situations, I was put in the same type store with my new company. I, again, worked hard to meet the expectations of my manager, the demands of the customers, and hit the company goals and targets, all at the expense of my own health and wellbeing.

As I was coming out of the fog of being a working mom with 2 little ones (only 16 months apart), I started to realize how important my health was and that I wasn't really doing anything to improve it. After having children, you have a different outlook on a lot of aspects in life. I wanted to have energy on my days off to run around with my kids. I wanted to live long enough to see my children enter the adult world and make something of themselves. Having children made me really want to be proactive towards my health. Being proactive is always my favorite approach in life. Being reactive just doesn't make any sense in my mind. When we know so much and have so many resources available to us today, being reactive just seems chaotic to me.

I knew I needed to get out of my current career path of community pharmacy and was able to join my husband in an independently owned long-term care pharmacy. I was able to actually take a lunch break and sit down. After working for 7 years with no breaks on shift, it was weird but exciting. This new job did not come without its own challenges, however, and as you probably know by now, I am not one to back down from a challenge. My stubbornness has not always served my health well. We grew a pharmacy from serving 200 beds to serving over 1500 beds, in just 2 years. We took on an untrained small staff, a large pharmacy automation process, and a lot of extra long days just to get the work done. That recipe of extra long days and too little help, combined with my determination to get it all done, was a recipe for disaster. Again, I found myself in a state of burnout.

All this time, I continued to go to my OBGYN and primary care doctor. My labs were "perfect" and my weight was "ideal." No issues at all and seemingly as healthy as they come. My exhaustion was from being a working mom while the migraines were fixed with a simple prescription. However, I had heart palpitations that were unexplained, but "not a big deal" because the cardiologist said my EKG, stress test, and echocardiogram showed no issues and therefore, I was dismissed. I was constantly thirsty, which was good, because I drank a lot of water each day, as everyone recommends. My post nasal drip was just allergies, and something to I could live with and could be fixed again with medicine. I had consistently been told that my constipation and mood swings were common for women. There was an answer, explanation, or pill for it all. I often heard phrases like, "It is common", "It's ok", or even "Here is a medicine to help." The sad part is, I actually believed them. These were the issues I had lived with for way too long.

In my quest to further my own health journey and find my own answers for feeling better, I went from one podcast to another during my daily commute to and from work. I finally stumbled upon Dr. Mark Hyman's podcast, *The Doctor's Farmacy*. I hadn't heard of functional medicine as an actual term and practice. I had heard things like, "eating asparagus fights off cancer" or "moving your phone out of the bed can help prevent cancer." What I didn't realize, however, was that what I was hearing and applying in small bits, was an aspect of just that, functional medicine.

Dr Hyman made a statement that really summed it all up for me. He said, "you are born with the genes you are given, but you don't have to express those genes." That was the statement I needed to hear, that made me a fan for life. I may carry the genes but I don't have to let them express themselves because I am in control! I can make a difference in how my health plays out for my future. This was especially important to me because cancer is very prevalent in my family. On my Dad's side we have my dad, my grandfather, and my great-grandmother and on my Mom's side, my mother, my grandmother, and my grandfather all with cancer diagnoses.

When listening to functional medicine podcasts, everything started to make sense! The functional medicine approach to healthcare was different from anything I had been a part of before. As I listened from one podcast to the next, I got so excited about being able to truly change a person's health trajectory. Of course, I started with myself and my husband. Dr. Mark Hyman would explain that food is medicine, health supplements can aid in symptom relief, and how diseases can be stopped and even reversed. It was a light bulb moment for me! Why didn't everyone use this approach to healthcare? Why wouldn't everyone be looking for the root causes instead of just isolated symptoms?

I have learned so much about myself through my practice of functional medicine. While taking the actions needed to take care of myself is not always easy, I have been able to take my health to the next level. I have significantly decreased inflammation in my body through diet changes and focusing on whole foods. I have also stopped taking allergy medication for my post nasal drip by cleaning up my diet and focusing on removing foods that I found I was sensitive (not allergic) too. I am healing my gut to allow for better tolerance and reintroduction of those foods. Through a stool analysis, I have found out I have dysbiosis of the gut, which is very common for Americans who grew up eating the standard American diet, and even more common for those with chronic stress. I now eat to fuel and feed my body instead of my emotions.

My biggest transformation has been through balancing my key nutrients. I took a Hair Tissue Mineral Analysis (HTMA) test and found the answer to so many of my issues. My migraines and my heart palpitations were brought on by lack of key nutrients in my body. Even though I ate healthy foods and prioritized my sleep, the chronic stress of the past 12 years had taken a toll on my body in unimaginable ways. My HTMA test showed copper toxicity, very low sodium and potassium, and low manganese, as well as ratio imbalances. On a seesaw scale where zero is the middle and represents perfect balance in the body, I was at a 4, the highest number. I was the seat on the far end of the seesaw, the furthest from being balanced and ready to fall off. At first glance of my results, I was so surprised! I carried no chronic diagnosis from a doctor. I saw only 1 specialist, my OBGYN, but the appointments were short and all tests came back as normal. I only had a prescription for birth control and migraines. I had a good BMI and people came to me for health related questions on a daily basis.

When I finally stopped and took a deeper look into my life and all the symptoms that I had just written off as part of being human, I realized how blessed I was to have found functional medicine. I have been able to find the root cause of some really important issues my body was having and was trying to warn me about all along. My body was telling me that I was not ok, but until this point I hadn't slowed down enough to listen to it. I truly feel that if I did not realize the root cause and work to reverse my nutrient imbalances, that soon enough my test at my annual physical would start to physically reflect negative health outcomes. There were many potential risks I faced like thyroid insufficiency, my adrenals would be shot, low immune function, the weight in the midsection (visceral fat) caused by blood sugar imbalances, and my body would be primed for a cancer diagnosis.

Now, I work regularly on decreasing my stress and simplifying my life so I can truly enjoy it. I have removed the word "hustle" from my motto and from my computer screen. A word that used to mean success to me has constantly gotten me into a state that does not and will not benefit me or my family. I am a work in progress but I have embraced words like deliberate and intentional, as well as phrases like, "work smarter, not harder." Functional medicine is what I thank for all these new realizations! My new lifestyle offers my mind more ease and my body is under so much less stress internally. I thought my stress was only an external factor, but now the internal impacts have been proven.

If everyone used this approach to healthcare, our population would have a completely different health outlook. If we educated those with symptoms on lifestyle modifications instead of prescribing more medication, what kind of world would we live in then? Think of how much better everyone would feel. If they felt better, they would be more kind. I know for a fact we could all use a little more kindness in our lives. I hope that one day functional medicine and conventional medicine are one. What a life people could live if our society combined the approach of lifestyle modifications first and foremost and then treat with medication as a last resort. This should be the standard of care.

Now, I have come to realize that all my previous experience was to help me learn, empathize, and better understand what so many go through. I have found a way to utilize all my knowledge and truly serve others by helping them understand the root cause of their issues. I have combined my passion and experience to found *Functionally Fit Rx*™. Now I help clients discover their own version of being "fit" using a functional medicine approach so that they can truly thrive. My passion is to help other healthcare professionals beat their exhaustion and burnout by inspiring them to take back control of their lives. Through my guidance, I empower them with the knowledge they need so they can continue healing and transforming the lives of all those they care for. That is the best way I can think of to help spread the word, through other healthcare professionals who experience the transformative power of functional medicine first hand. I know how essential our healthcare providers are and know they need to be taken care of just as much as they take care of others. My goal is to leave a lasting impression on all those I meet, to inspire them to want to make healthier choices and continue to pass along their knowledge, too. This is my legacy.

ABOUT DR. PANA NINAN

D r. Pana Ninan is a Certified Functional Medicine Specialist™ from
The STORRIE™ Institute, Pharmacist, mom of 2, and warrior for
women. She has been published in multiple online articles such as Authority magazine, Thrive Global, and Yahoo!. Dr. Pana is also a virtual
summit speaker and a frequent podcast guest.

For more than 12 years, she has worked professionally in both the
community and long-term care setting where she is known for her knowledge and ability to teach, working as a trainer, educator, and preceptor for
her coworkers, patients, and students respectively. Working in the long-
term care setting, Dr. Pana realized her passion for helping protect others
from the long-term effects of poor health habits and the compounding
side effects of taking multiple medications.

Dr. Pana has taken her passions of helping people heal and feeling
their best to become founder and CEO, *Functionally Fit Rx, LLC* where
she works with driven women in healthcare to conquer their exhaustion
and burnout through her signature *SPARK Method*: focusing on stress
management, purification + cleansing, assess labs, routines + habits, and

nutrition. She understands the importance of mindset, building healthy habits, and addressing the root cause of symptoms.

Dr. Pana is passionate about helping women overcome their health struggles and determine their own version of fit. She does this by empowering them with knowledge and inspiring them to take control and transform their lives using a functional medicine approach.

www.drpananinan.com | pana@functionallyfitrx.com | IG: functionallyfitrx

Chapter 14

BREAKING DOWN "THE WALL"

By: Dr. Radka Toms, MD

"It is only with the heart that one can see rightly;
what is essential is invisible to the eye."

– Antoine de Saint-Exupery

I was born on a perfect sunny day, just four months too late. Let me explain. Four months before I was born, Czechoslovakia played its first game against England in the European Cup at Wembley. The Czechoslovak team went on, after more than a year, to win the 1976 European Cup against West Germany in a nail-biting final that went to penalties. Antonin Panenka scored the winning goal. It is the only time Czechoslovakia has ever won the European Cup. Perhaps you find it curious that I should mention such an event. You see, I am Czech, and I am very proud of my country. Prague is the capital, with its world-famous Charles Bridge and the beautiful mountains and valleys of Bohemia and Moravia. The Prague Spring of 1968 was when the people of my country rose up against Soviet tyranny, despite the terrible consequences. All this to say, to the Czechs, winning the European Cup was perhaps the best thing to happen to our country during this time. It spelled out hope.

February 7th, 1975 I was born in a small town in the Czech Republic to a very close family consisting of my grandparents, parents, my younger sister, and I. My grandfather was a dentist. He had a very successful private practice before the Communists took over. The communists did not want entrepreneurs to exist at all, and much less well-to-do entrepreneurs. They wanted Communist card carriers, and my grandparents and parents could not bring themselves to comply.

We lived simply but had everything we needed. We grew fruit and vegetables in our small garden and my grandfather fixed teeth on a small wooden adjustable piano stool in the kitchen, the dentist's drill hanging from the fridge. People were grateful and showered us with eggs, hams, chickens, sausages, and sometimes even fish from the Oxbow Lakes of the Oder.

While my grandfather and father instilled in us the value of honesty, community, and hard work, my grandmother and mother used to regale us with Czech wisdom, little local proverbs that have stayed with me all my life. My grandmother used to say, "Veselá mysl je pul zdraví" or "Happiness is half of health." My mother worked in an orphanage and witnessed terrible family tragedies. One day, she took me and my sister aside, ushered us into the little pantry, and said, "Rodina je jedním z mistrovských děl přírody" or "The family is one of nature's masterpieces" and impressed upon us that no matter what, always to treasure the family we have and in due course, we would too, become mothers. Oh, how I treasured our close family. I never, even once, felt we were lacking in anything, even though West Germany, far, far to our west it was said that there was a Disneyland of plenty. They had Mercedes and BMWs – and we had Škodas and Trabants. But what did it matter?

In 1989, the Berlin Wall came down. Mikhail Gorbachev appeared on television one year later to dissolve the Soviet Union, admitting that the Communist system did not work. Of course, it didn't work. We knew it didn't work. We Czechs had suffered the consequences. The communist system had irreparably blighted the lives of my grandparents and parents. There was nothing that could be done to fix the damage from the past, but they could do everything in their power to offer my younger sister and me a better life.

When I was 14 I started attending a boarding school and began studying pharmacy. I worked hard. And before long my longtime dream to live in Prague, a dream of mine since the age of twelve, came true. I was selected, at the age of eighteen, to study medicine at Charles University in Prague. I walked along the fourteenth century gothic Charles Bridge, rubbed the lucky bronze statue of St. John Nepomuk, and placed my hand on his bronze cross to make my wishes come true – To be a great doctor and one day, a good mother. My grandparents and parents were so proud. I was in Prague for twelve years. I studied medicine and I worked night and day in the General Teaching University Hospital in Prague. I was so happy. I was helping people, just as my parents and grandparents had done. I felt I at least owed them that.

Unfortunately, my mother passed away in her forties after suffering from cancer for two years, I was devastated. My father, sister, and I were there by her bedside. She died on Christmas Day. I watched the light go out from her eyes. I committed to becoming a medical doctor, and that's just what I did. It was Professor Martin Filipec whom I met in medical school, that inspired me to become an Ophthalmologist. As a cataract surgeon today, I can have an immediate positive impact on my patient's vision and change their quality of life dramatically. It's a very rewarding and special field of medicine.

Ophthalmology is the science of the eyes or "the windows to the soul", as William Shakespeare put it. I put all my energies into helping people at the hospital. Night and day. Ninety hours a week. I never stopped. Perhaps it was my desperate way of trying to save my mother and make up for my parents' and grandparents' blighted past. Eventually, however, I hit "The Wall".

"The Wall" I'm referring to is when your body breaks down. You've been pumping it with coffee, sugar, and chocolate, anything that will keep you going on next to no sleep. I was in a perpetual state of stress, fatigue, and exhaustion. I was in collapse. My face exploded with rosacea. I began to lose focus in my eyes. I wasn't helping anyone in the hospital considering the state I was in. So naturally, I knew I had to do something to make a change. I dived into research and started studying everything about the gut microbiome, nutrition, functional medicine, the "power of mindset", autophagy, inflammation, family constellation, yoga, meditation, breathing, spontaneous remissions, mitochondrial and hormonal health.

I couldn't stop reading. I needed to know what could I do to heal myself. Actually, I was looking for scientific proof that I could indeed "heal myself." Who was it who said, "Physician, heal thyself"? Anyways, I came across the Institute of Functional Medicine and I watched Dr. Mark Hyman's 2010 TedTalk about functional medicine over again and over again. I read quizzically, Professor Lustig's paper linking sugar directly to inflammation. Sugar? Surely not. It was in everything.

I didn't know the term "functional medicine" ten years ago. As a medical doctor, I just think in terms of biochemical pathways. Before long, though, it dawned on me. Most of the biochemical pathways that control homeostasis are controlled by nutrition. Was nutrition the answer? Could you actually "help yourself to health"?

This is when I began cataloging the foods I was eating. I researched the gut microbiome and its association with various health issues. I found that my diet was low in fiber and unvaried. I increased my vegetable consumption to the point that the crisper (refrigerator) drawers couldn't hold my weekly shopping. I aimed to eat half a kilo of vegetables and fruit a day. I kept meat in my diet but complemented it with nuts and seeds, my primary source of protein, together with some lentils and beans. In a few months' time, I had created an entire anti-inflammatory diet that I called Judy Garland's "Rainbow".

I completely cut out refined sugar. That's right, I cut out all refined flour, soy products, packaged foods, alcohol, and limited my dairy consumption. I ate a rainbow of colorful vegetables full of healing phytochemicals packed with polyphenols, naturally occurring plant chemicals, and biologically active compounds in plants that would have made Judy Garland proud. I started practicing yoga and breathing techniques, and on occasion, even fasted.

Slowly but surely, "The Wall" came down, brick by brick, just as the Berlin Wall had done. My Rosacea disappeared within months and never returned. I was finally feeling better. My mind, body, and soul felt aligned.

Everything was going well for a while before it wasn't. Suddenly, I had a crisis of conscience. My crisis of conscience came from a realization that the medicine I was practicing so conscientiously addressed the symptoms of ill-health, but not the root causes. As doctors, as professionals, we treat chronic diseases in silos. We treat illnesses such as macular degeneration, glaucoma, dementia, cancer, high blood pressure, but we are treating the end stage of the process. Much of the time, we are not even looking at the cause.

Here's the deal, we are but pallbearers of the body. So, in tribute to my mother, I made a deliberate decision to step over "The Wall" and delve into "The Body." I found it ironic that my twelve years of study had equipped me with an encyclopedic knowledge of the body but, even so, I knew very little about how it actually worked, how it balanced, how it's possible to achieve the "Yin and Yang." I realized that this was precisely what the practitioners of "functional medicine" were trying to tell us. They were telling us that chronic diseases can be stopped and, in some cases, can even be reversed.

This realization is what led me to create *MySugarStop*™. *MySugarStop*™ is helping people to improve their metabolic health so they can become healthier and feel happier. It was when I realized that the most major contributor to ill-health is sugar. It is well known that diabetes, cardiovascular disease, high blood pressure, rheumatoid arthritis, dry eye, and macular degeneration are inflammatory disorders. There's clear, irrefutable evidence that nutrition influences our overall health in a very significant way. And sugar is a big contributing culprit. All of my learning and experience went into *MySugarStop*™.

The initiative blossomed over the years with the principles of functional medicine that I continued to learn and apply. I evangelized and found myself consistently encouraging people to alter their eating and lifestyle behavior. I talked to them about the path towards becoming healthier and happier.

During my time working as an eye surgeon, I will never forget a patient in the eye clinic who came to see me for a check-up after six months. He was 30 kilos lighter, his diabetes had improved, his blood pressure was down and he came to me with a smile on his face. I said, wow, your results are fantastic! What did you do? And he said, "I did exactly what you suggested." I stared at him. My jaw dropped. It really worked!

I was so happy. I was fulfilling my grandparent's dream. I was *really* helping people. My studies in ophthalmology were key to helping.

There's a quote from Saint Jerome, one of the early Church Fathers, that I particularly like:

> *"The face is the mirror of the mind, while the eyes, without speaking, confess the secrets of the heart."*
>
> – SAINT JEROME

The eye, you see, is a fascinating organ. It is the only place in the human body where part of your central nervous system is visible. We often see clues in the eyes that indicate health issues elsewhere in your body. Ophthalmologists are sometimes the first to diagnose a medical condition because the first signs of certain diseases appear in the eye. The retina, the back of the eye, is a very sensitive indicator of health and nutrition. It is perhaps the most metabolically active tissue per unit weight in the body. And clearly, it has the largest blood supply per unit weight.

It was clear to me that if I wanted to influence my patient's vision, I had to impact their overall health. I discussed that with every patient, every single time they came to the clinic. As you can imagine, however, in a twelve-minute appointment where I only saw them periodically, I couldn't help them in the significant way I really wanted to. I knew they would have to change their habits and improve their nutrition in order to improve their overall health.

I knew what I wanted. I wanted to offer long-term solutions. I wanted to help people improve their metabolic health, give them tools, support, and guidance, and teach them how to use food as medicine so that they can be well and see well. I wanted my patients "to help themselves to health" just the way I had done as a physician.

This now is my mission. *"Helping People to Health"* through the programs I have designed to help others achieve tangible results. That is the purpose of *MySugarStop*™. No, it's not just about stopping sugar. It is about pursuing a nutritional diet and lifestyle that help you to be a happier, healthier individual. And it does not stop there.

As my grandmother said, *"Happiness is half of health."* Being a happy mother, I can influence the treasure and blessing of a happier, healthier family. I have been blessed. Perhaps St. John of Nepomuk, really was listening all those years ago when I walked along the Charles Bridge. I married an adorable Englishman. He has a tiny gap between his front two teeth that my grandfather would, no doubt, have fixed. I find it charming, however.

I have traveled the world with him, to England, to Australia, to the United States, to Germany where my two beautiful daughters, Sophia and Charlotte were born. My *SugarStop™* helps me to be the mother I want to be. *"Musite bránit svou rodinu"* or *"You have to defend your family,"* was another cherished thing my grandmother said.

And a healthy mother is perhaps the best defense of all. I still go back to the family house in Valasske Mezirici, in the beautiful valley Beskydy in the Czech Republic. The apple and cherry trees are still there. There's even a Feng Shui garden which my father likes to sit in. The vegetable garden still brings forth lettuce, beans, and onions.

My father is proud of me.

He knows that his daughter, as a functional medicine practitioner, has changed the lives of many, enabling them to live better, see better and enjoy more fulfilling lives with their families.

It's what he wanted for me, all those years ago.

We look together at the pink blossoms on the trees. I hold his hand in mine.

And perhaps now, I am proud of myself.

ABOUT DR. RADKA TOMS

Dr. Radka Toms is a Licensed Medical Doctor, Ophthalmologist, Functional Medicine Practitioner, Integrative Nutrition Health Coach, and published contributor in medical journals. Dr. Radka is also a Philanthropist, Author, and mother of two beautiful children. Her expertise has been featured in podcasts, summits, and a variety of professional webinars.

She is the founder and CEO of *MySugarStop*™ which helps women and men around the world improve their metabolic health, gut health, gain energy, and lose their stubborn weight, using the philosophy "let food be the medicine", and empowering people towards a self-healing journey so that they can be more energized, feel healthier and happier.

Dr. Radka's greatest passions are being an eye surgeon, with a sub-specialty in glaucoma, cornea, cataract surgery, and functional medicine practitioner with a focus on Nutritional Ophthalmology and Rosacea Healing. Going forward, Dr. Radka is committed to continuing to transform people's lives.

Dr. Radka is on the mission to provide support and education to help people identify the "root cause" of their illnesses, and get answers on their challenges to create healing so that they can feel healthier, happier, and live joyful lives.

www.mysugarstop.com | Radka@mysugarstop.com |
Instagram: @dr.radka.toms | Instagram: @rosacea_healing

Chapter 15

IS THERE NOT A CAUSE?

By: Dr. Rose N. Ngishu, MD, CFMS

*"Dear friend, I pray that you may enjoy good health and that all may
go well with you, even as your soul is getting along well."*

– 3 John 1:2 NIV

In 1948, the World Health Organization defined health as, "a state of
complete physical, mental, and social well-being and not merely the
absence of disease or infirmity." Unfortunately, many of us still lose our
health insidiously, long before disease, illness, or infirmity ever sets in.
Often, it is not until a disease set's in, that we begin to pay attention to
our health. It is time for a paradigm shift and a complete overhaul in our
approach to health and wellness.

Many have asked me why, as a well-trained, board-certified, thriving
internal medicine physician, I would decide to get into functional medicine, rather than just stay in my lane of conventional medicine. Well,
the answer is simple. It all comes down to the question of, "Is there not
a cause?" In the US, we are spending more on health care for one person
than we are on feeding an average family for the entire year, is there not
a cause? One major cause of bankruptcy in America today is medical
expenses, is there not a cause? In spite of all that expenditure, people still

find themselves feeling unwell and chronically stressed. We rank poorly as a nation in key health outcome metrics compared to other developed nations, so I ask again, is there not a cause? The modern diet is the central driving force behind 672,000 deaths annually in the US, and more than 11 million worldwide,[1] is there not a cause?

It is for these reasons, and many more, that I am honing into functional and lifestyle medicine. In health coaching and consulting, I am beginning to make a dent in this mammoth of a health crisis. Frankly, the question of why got into functional medicine is, at best, shallow, and at worst, disappointing. It speaks volumes of how deeply we are out of touch with ageless common sense, priceless wisdom, and health practices of our ancestors, in the name of modern life. Of course, times are different, and the challenges of modern life are unique to us. However, we are still the best-preserved specimen of the human genetic code. So what is it that has failed us, compared to Methuselah from the Old Testament of the Bible, who without an Aspirin, a statin, or a single man-made by-pass graft in his body lived to be 969 years of age?

Don't get me wrong, I love the conveniences of modern life. I love western medicine too, but only when utilized adjunctively. I practice it prudently. It saves lives! Especially for acute illnesses, such as infections and trauma. It prolongs the lifespan, somewhat, for so many with chronic conditions such as heart disease and cancer, who until very recently would have died much earlier. The issue is, modern life and medicine put no real vitality and health into the years it can add to people's lives. Furthermore, they come at a price tag only few can really afford. At the rate we have been going, things are unsustainable! For the most part, we are at a point of diminishing returns. No matter how much we continue to invest into them, things are proving to be less and less fulfilling for both creators and consumers, patients and practitioners. Not to mention some of the outright harm that has come to the environment consequently. All of this is compiling and is leaving our world worse for future generations than what we started with.

As a generally responsible person and scientist at heart, I have to look deeper and further to see how I can do my part to help. Through study and observation, I have arrived at functional and lifestyle medicine. Beyond conventional medicine, is this quest of getting to the root causes of disease and illnesses. There are propositions for effective and sustainable holistic approaches to health and wellness. Motivations for healthy behavior change, where health and wellness can truly be restored and maintained in an impactful and sustainable way. I believe in functional and lifestyle medicine.

From the age of seven, all I wanted to be was a physician, in that seemingly Godforsaken place. I grew up in a rural, western Kenya village called Malomonye. I wanted to be the "doctor where there is no doctor," in part because I had asthma, that remained undiagnosed and untreated for a long time. I remember having many attacks often, with chest tightness and barely breathing. Thankfully I never completely closed off my airway. I had a chronic cough, and one of my teachers would later scold me for always clearing my throat. My grandmother and parents would boil some herbs, and make me inhale the bitter vapors for some relief. Honestly, I am here today, because it is not all about western medicine. The inspiration to be a physician was also in part from an old manual titled, *Where There Is No Doctor: A Village Health Care Handbook,* published by Hesperian Health Guides. I do not know where my mom got it from, but she was a school teacher and later became a doctor and counselor in our village. It was mostly a guide on first-aid, for burns, diarrhea, and many other common issues. Mother would refer to it every so often. She'd incorporate its guidance, along with her general knowledge and wisdom about traditional remedies, to help a neighbor or a child at school or even us at home. Sometimes it would be in the middle of the night, in a village without a hospital, midwife, or even transportation to a medical facility. This was life for me growing up. What I have learned was that this was functional medicine, only in different terms and in a different setting. My parents were, and still remain, very resourceful to their community. From education, preventive health, coaching, and even spiritual care. They farmed, so we ate a variety of fresh farm produce. From pumpkin leaves to taro roots to homemade bone broth. Little did I know at the time, what I was putting in my body was actually gold for my health.

In 1998 at 20 years old, I started my new life in the United States without any family around and with very little money. I quickly learned that pursuing my childhood dream was not going to be easy. I was not going to get any more money from home, so I had to get a job. That wasn't easy, either. Suffice it to say, working full-time at a minimum wage job, hardly paid enough for moderate sustenance, much less for a college education. I worked two jobs and went to school full-time, sometimes taking 17 to 18 credit hours per semester. I was disappointed to learn that I needed an undergraduate degree before going to medical school. In my disappointment, I picked nursing again, because it was the closest thing to what I wanted to do. By God's grace, I got my associate's, then my bachelor's degree, and eventually graduated with honors.

I worked in the critical care areas, then briefly in administration and outpatient. I started a family and school went on the back burner for a while. I even contemplated not going back, but I knew in my heart of hearts that everything else I did was going to be my second best. Nothing wrong with settling for the second-best, if that's truly all you can do. For me, though, that was a daunting idea. I just knew I still needed to proceed to medical school. It wasn't until the healthcare environment I was working in became more hostile than I could bear, that I knew I had to make a change. At the time, the economy was hurting, patients were sicker than ever and were presenting late with complications and we had staffing shortages. It was terrible. I mean, I can't tell you how much I hated those calls around 5 AM, asking if I wanted to, "pick up an extra shift." Yet, those proverbial "Egyptian Masters" only expected us to deliver fast, quality, cost-effective care, regardless of the diminishing resources and support. I cried often, especially when I felt rushed and had not done all I wanted to do to help my patients. I just knew I could not remain in that position. Amidst all these, I developed food intolerances to just about anything and everything. I was not sure why, but now I do, at least in part.

I made the hard decision to return to school. We had four young children, the last one still in diapers. My husband was out of work too, but that's a story for another day. Medical school was quite enjoyable for me, even though I missed out on the parties and most of the extracurricular stuff because I spared that time for my family. I had to remain focused. Things were tough, but I graduated on time and even earned an induction into the medical honor society. I also completed my interim medicine specialty residency training. For a while, I considered a subspecialty in cardiology, nephrology, endocrinology, and had finally settled on hematology-oncology. Towards the end of my second year in residency, I had my own serious medical illness arise. Thyroid problems, anemia, depression, pain, you name it. I even had to have a hysterectomy. I am so glad I had already finished having children at that time.

After much prayer and reflection, I found real peace, specializing in general internal medicine primary care. The challenging and stimulating clinical cases are just the right mix for me. The variety of conditions is fascinating and what I love most is the privilege to do the initial workup before referring to other specialists as may be necessary. I love this that I do, and I love seeing my patients and clients feel better.

I wish I could say all my patients are better. Unfortunately, there is a sizable proportion of them that don't seem to be. Again, I have to look deeper, to be able to truly help them heal. If numbers don't lie, we have some staggering statistics that demand our attention. 60% of Americans have at least one chronic medical condition. 40% have two or more chronic medical illnesses. At least 89% of patients hospitalized for the Covid-19 virus have an underlying medical problem. The Center for Disease Control (CDC) estimates that at least 90% of our healthcare spending goes towards treating chronic diseases. Globally, at least one billion people worldwide have a chronic medical condition.

So, how do we help these patients? There's some good news, again, from the functional and lifestyle medicine space. Up to 80% of all chronic diseases can be reversed if we apply what we know about lifestyle and health. The question is, why haven't we?

Part of the problem is the assertion, by some of the powers that be, that functional medicine is not sufficiently empirical science. Well, who do you think determines what is plausible empirical science? Spoiler Alert – It's the same economic profiteers of a broken, better yet, sick, healthcare system. And who is to claim that conventional medicine is perfect? I work in it and I'll tell us all for free, it is not perfect science either. To be clear, conventional medicine has served its purpose, but it is ill-equipped to manage any chronic disease effectively and sustainably. It has definitely ushered us into the era Thomas Edison spoke of in 1902 when he said:

"The doctor of the future will give no medicine, but will instruct his (or her) patients in the care of the human frame, in diet,

and in the cure and prevention of disease."

That future is here, it has been here all along. That doctor envisioned by Thomas Edison is a functional and lifestyle medicine specialist. Equipped with timeless, effective, and sustainable principles to restore vitality to the human experience, beyond the limitations of conventional medicine. With so many opposing and intimidating giants in the way, I ask you, "Is there not a cause for functional medicine?" I am seeing good results with my motivated patients and clients. For those who are yet to be motivated, or are still stuck in the old thinking process, I still do my best to try to point them in the right direction. Otherwise, this train has left the station and it is not stopping.

Outside my conventional practice, I have a functional, lifestyle, and wellness coaching practice where I help my clients release all forms of toxic stress and equip them for optimum health, energy, longevity, and passion otherwise known as *HELP.* If you are a motivated female in a high-stress profession, I got your back. I understand that women in this set of circumstances have special needs that are often misunderstood by the larger community. They are highly driven, compassionate, and unfortunately, oftentimes sacrifice themselves and their health in order to help others. They hardly have time for their own self-care, and the issues are even more complex if they are immigrants or belong to a minority group. As women, we know we have to tough it out no matter what, but with that comes a tremendous amount of stress.

It is critically important to address stress because 70-90% of primary health complaints are due to stress. Stress is where most people lose their health so insidiously. I have walked down that path, in those shoes, and now I take care of those feeling overwhelmed and stressed. I coach and guide them to great health, high energy, longevity, and the ongoing pursuit of their passions. I help them to switch off when they arrive at home in order to be fully present with their loved ones. In my practice, I offer specific functional testing as well and create personalized interventions to resolve the underlying issues. One of the best parts is that we can do all of this virtually, so you don't have to be local to work with me. If you struggle with a chronic medical problem, toxic stress, overwhelm, or find yourself feeling lost and unregulated, you owe it to yourself to reach out. I am here, ready and waiting to help you find true healing. I am on a mission to help others overcome stress and experience real wellness, starting from within.

"Giving someone power is better than giving them a pill."

— DR. DEAN ORNISH

References:

1. The Lancet. (2019, April 24). *Health effects of dietary risks in 195 countries, 1990–2017: a systematic analysis for the Global Burden of Disease Study 2017.* Health effects of dietary risks in 195 countries.

2. Buttorff, C., Ruder, T., & Bauman, M. (2017, May 31). *Multiple Chronic Conditions in the United States | RAND.* RAND Corporation. Retrieved from https://www.rand.org/pubs/tools/TL221.html

3. Centers for Disease Control and Prevention. (2020, April 17). *Hospitalization Rates and Characteristics of Patients Hospitalized with Laboratory-Confirmed Coronavirus Disease 2019 — COVID-NET, 14 States, March 1–30, 2020 | MMWR.* CDC. Retrieved from https://www.cdc.gov/mmwr/volumes/69/wr/mm6915e3.htm

4. Hajat, C., & Stein, E. (2018, 12 1). *The global burden of multiple chronic conditions: A narrative review.* Elsevier. https://www.ncbi.nlm.nih.gov/pmc/articles/PMC6214883/pdf/main.pdf

5. Healio. (2017, May 26). *Primary care physicians can help prevent, reverse cardiovascular disease.* Healio Primary Care. https://www. healio.com/news/primary-care/20170525/primary-care-physicians-can-help-prevent-reverse-cardiovascular-diseases

6. London School of Hygiene And Tropical Medicine. (2020, June 16). *Estimates suggest one in five people worldwide have an underlying health condition that could increase their risk of severe COVID-19 if infected | LSHTM.* The London School of Hygiene & Tropical Medicine. Retrieved from https://www.lshtm.ac.uk/newsevents/news/2020/estimates-suggest-one-five-people-worldwide-have-underlying-health-condition

7. Lifestyle Medicine Research Summit. (2020, December 22). *Prioritized Research for the Prevention, Treatment, and Reversal of Chronic Disease: Recommendations From the Lifestyle Medicine Research Summit.* Frontiers in Medicine. Retrieved from https://www.frontiersin. org/articles/10.3389/fmed.2020.585744/full

8. Ornish, D., Brown, S.E., Billings, J.H., Scherwitz, L.W., & Ports, T.A. (2020, June 16). *Estimates suggest one in five people worldwide have an underlying health condition that could increase their risk of severe COVID-19 if infected | LSHTM.* The London School of Hygiene & Tropical Medicine. Retrieved from https://www.lshtm.ac.uk/newsevents/news/2020/estimates-suggest-one-five-people-worldwide-have-underlying-health-condition

9. Sagner, M., Katz, D., Lianov, L., Braman, M., Behbod, B., Dysinger, W., & Ornish, D. (2014, October 27). *Lifestyle medicine potential for reversing a world of chronic disease epidemics: from cell to community.*

The Internal Journal of Clinical Practice. https://onlinelibrary.wiley.com/doi/full/10.1111/ijcp.12509

ABOUT DR. ROSE NGISHU

Dr. Rose Ngishu is a Board Certified Internal Medicine Specialist working in full-time clinical practice. She is a Certified Functional Medicine Specialist™ from The STORRIE™ Institute and has a special interest and training in lifestyle medicine, functional medicine, and financial coaching. She was a Registered Nurse for 15 years, before which she was a certified nurse's assistant for three years. She has since retired from these two roles. She is married and has four amazing children. Dr. Rose finds joy through being a singer, song-writer, poet, entrepreneur, speaker, and author.

As a female immigrant, Dr. Rose fully understands the challenges of living below the poverty line, which in itself can have a negative impact on health and longevity. As life would have it, she found herself being the primary breadwinner for her family, which was a role she loved but brought with it a load of chronic stress and health. She has learned to overcome that stress, and its negative impact on her health, mostly through the principles of holistic health.

Currently, she is seeing her patients reverse some of their chronic conditions just by incorporating the principles of lifestyle and functional medicine as she teaches them. Drawing from her own professional and personal experience she has created a program to help female primary breadwinners in high-stress professions, and with competing caretaker obligations, who are feeling tired, overwhelmed, and anxious, to release the stress, so that they can enjoy great health, high energy, and switch off from work and be present with their loved ones once at home. She encourages people to continue to pursue their vocational and/or recreational passions, as they should not be compromised because of busy schedules. Dr. Rose is not seeking to replace your primary care doctor, rather, to augment your wellness to bring you peace. She is on a mission to help others be whole.

Dr. Rose believes that wholesome health is key to enjoying one's life, most of which can be achieved without expensive medications and conventional medical procedures. Of course that has its own place in this world, however, it should not be the mainstay. She also believes that financial well-being should be a part of the holistic approach because money touches everything we do and become. Because of these beliefs, she incorporates financial literacy into her program, aiming to remove every barrier to wellness, growth, and longevity. If you are a female primary breadwinner, and you are ready to optimize your health, escape the debilitating ramifications of chronic stress, please reach out Dr. Rose Ngishu so she can guide you towards a life of peace and freedom.

www.drrosengishu.com | Instagram: @rnngishu |
LinkedIn: Rose Ngishu, MD

Made in United States
North Haven, CT
05 April 2022